*Some Psychological Aspects
of Religious Education*

Some Psychological Aspects of Religious Education

A Deus Books Edition of the Paulist Press, 1961, by special arrangement with P. J. Kenedy & Sons, New York, N. Y.

Nihil Obstat: John A. Goodwine, J. C. D., *Censor Librorum*.

Imprimatur: ✠ Francis Cardinal Spellman,
Archbishop of New York.

New York, August 31, 1959.

Abbé

Marc Oraison, D.D., M.D.

Love or
Constraint?

Translated from the French
By Una Morrissey, B.A.

DEUS BOOKS
PAULIST PRESS (Paulist Fathers)
Glen Rock, N. J.

Contents

© 1959 by P. J. Kenedy & Sons, New York.

Deus Books Edition © 1961 by
The Missionary Society of St. Paul the Apostle
in the State of New York.

Library of Congress Catalog Card Number: 59-12899

Manufactured in the United States of America

Introduction

To attempt the creation of a new outlook on the problem of religious education may appear presumptuous or even futile. The subject is one so very well regulated by tradition and custom that it would seem there is nothing in it to change; the situation that actually prevails, however, impels us to believe that there is. Many educators have already realized this, and the movement during recent years to revise the catechism is a further proof. Moreover, one need only take stock of the feeble results on the strictly religious plane too often produced by education called Christian. It is regrettable, for example, to encounter orthodox believers, persons of the highest culture but whose religious thought has remained practically infantile, retaining a sort of retarded development in their spiritual outlook that prevents them from becoming vital and effective witnesses of Jesus Christ.

Quite certainly it is not the religious doctrine that needs to be recast and, in any event, we should not be capable of this: it does not originate with us; it is, one might say, the confidential communication of the Infinite Love that created us, instructs us and saves

us. We cannot modify or remake the light of the sun.
. . . But it could be useful from time to time to give
fresh thought to the manner in which we expose ourselves to it so that it may be of vital use to us since
that is its true purpose. If God has created us thinking beings, it is for us to think, under the penalty of
failing Him in what He expects of us, and our receptivity to His Word of life depends in part upon ourselves. At least it seems necessary that we ourselves
should oppose no obstacle to it. This is the matter to
which we will give thought in the course of this
present work: Are the methods of education from the
religious point of view suitably adapted at this period
of the world's history to their special work of bringing
humanity into the presence of the Divinity? Might
we not, perhaps, suggest that some "tactical errors"
have inadvertently crept in; that there are omissions
and even obscurities; that, despite the best good will
and sometimes even in the course of good intentions,
there obtains, nevertheless, a rigidity and over-all
monotony that is actually redolent of the spirit of
evil?

If there is one word which, above all others, is
equivocal in its definition, it is surely the word "tradition." In Catholic parlance it is used technically
to designate the transcendent teaching of the Church.
In this context the word is in the singular and carries
an initial capital. But in the common language of
the day the word tradition signifies habits of thought
or of action or behavior inherited from previous gener-
ations, and in this context it is put into the plural
and keeps a small initial letter. These two senses of
the one word are completely different and it is absolutely essential not to confuse them. Yet this confusion occurs very frequently and it is a continual and
highly difficult task to separate the two meanings in
people's minds. For example, the Real Presence in
the Holy Eucharist and the sacrificial character of the

Mass are a part of Tradition, while many of the liturgical details of the celebration of the Holy Sacrifice are no more than traditions, that is to say, they are not essential to the Mass, and the Church could change or modify any of them if she so desired. It is part of the nature of the Church, in fact, to be a living organism, not something mummified or fossilized, and to live a full life shared by all her members in unity and under the direction of her hierarchy.

Some regrettable confusions have crept into methods of religious education which have resulted in children believing that some quite pointless detail is a part of the unchanging essentials of our faith. Without wishing to be uncompromisingly critical, we might be permitted to think that this is happening all too often. On the other hand, there is no need for anyone to be surprised or scandalized by a process that is as old as humanity itself and one of which religious history has given us many examples.

The Jewish people, for instance, under the influence of Revelation, through the teaching of the Prophets, accepted an existential contract with God. This came to assume a form in various ceremonial rites and habits of behavior deriving directly from these rites. But gradually these rites and practices took firm root in the psychology and the conventions of the Jews, and showed a tendency to exist on their own account and even to take the place of what they merely signified. It is the weakness of human nature that it can seldom maintain its relationship with the living Mystery in a pure state. The satisfaction derived from having performed such-and-such a rite or having observed externally this or that precept, will always get in the way of the true search for Him whom one can never fully discover. Ritualism and formalism will imperceptibly take the place of a religion that is no longer more than a pretense or a form of behavior. And when God shall speak again—through His Prophets or through His Word, as the Epistle to the Hebrews tells us—the men who are faithful to their rites but who have lost the spirit that gives such rites their meaning will not be ready to follow Him. That, in fact, is exactly what befell the Pharisees, and it is that which explains their conflict, violent and yet genuine, with Christ, the "Nonconformist."

This process of mummification, or ritualistic-moralistic mechanization, is by no means an extra-ordinary phenomenon in religious history. On the contrary, it is a persistent characteristic. Herein, in fact, is to be found the whole story of the sustained opposition between the entire line of prophets preparing for and leading up to the coming of the Redeemer and the succession of ritualists ending in the Pharisees and finally the cabala.

Throughout the history of the Catholic Church the process has repeated itself. The outburst of the "Reformation," even though directed by the over-weening pride of Luther, and for that reason transformed into a revolt, found its origin in the profound need of men to find again the authentic religious meaning of the Mystery of God and of the Faith. Despite the impact on his life of this Mystery, man always retains the tendency to return gradually to the mentality of the primitive who believes in magic; and this is true of him even in epochs considered most "enlightened" and most devoted to rationalism, as is shown by the vogue for faith-healers, fortunetellers and other sorts of false mystics so prevalent in our twentieth century. This clinging to the rite for its own sake, or to the observance of the letter of the law simply for its own sake, is without any doubt the most subtle, because it is the most cunningly dis-guised, enemy of true religious sentiment. It is also ineradicable, and the main point is to make every effort to ensure that the faithful shall not be its vic-tims. We must do everything in our power to make certain that the source of truth shall not be hidden under an accumulation of dead leaves. True life must be found again behind a façade of mechanical habits.

The times in which we live possess at least the advantage of being filled with a most earnest and ardent desire for truth and for life. It is generally realized that much plaster has to be scraped away in order to reveal the original Roman arches buried beneath the accumulated by-products of a religious sentimentality bordering on fetishism. Just so is it also realized that a great many habits falsely termed "educational" should be revised, especially in regard to that part of education that is concerned with preparing and developing the young human being for his meeting with God. Just as something unsightly or offensive to the eye ends by becoming intolerable, so also do some forms of incoherence or inadequacy in religious education become so. Before the drama of a world searching for God in the midst of a darkness particularly impenetrable and agonizing we, as Christians, can no longer tolerate the existence of certain authoritarian educational patterns, whether clerical or moralist in origin.

The progress made in the study of psychology helps us here. If Freud was able to say that religion was simply a superior form of neurosis, it was possibly because the method of presenting religion — and we speak here of education regarded as Christian—betrayed its subject rather than serving it. During the course of the centuries psychology remained at the level of an oversimplified and idealistic explanation of reality. We might search back through the mists of history for the causes of such blindness so grievously exposed at the time of the upheaval most inappropriately termed the Renaissance. But that would take us outside the scope of our argument. The fact is simply this: methodical and objective study of practical human psychology demonstrates in a particularly impressive manner the progressively and positively frighteningly dehumanizing effect of religious education along the lines bequeathed to us by the most worn-out and futile so-called "traditions."

It is not really surprising that intolerable conflicts, inescapable contradictions and "loss of faith" so often arise from this state of affairs, for such tragic results are nothing more nor less than the scandalized refusal of the human mind to accept pharisaical ritualism instead of living religion. Not the least of the scandal is owing to the fact that people with the best intentions persist grimly in clinging to these pseudo "traditions" and blindly divorce the work from God. If this work of religious education is directed toward man with the intention of enlightening and redeeming him, obviously it must be directed toward man as he really is. There can be no contradiction between Revelation and all that scientific research teaches us about mankind. Therefore, from the point of view that forms the argument and theme of this book it seems a matter of urgency that every effort should be made to bring both of these forms of knowledge face to face in a complementary and not in an antagonistic spirit.

Modern psychology has brought to light two points which in effect had been forgotten. The first point is that the human being, who is before all else a particular individual and not a metaphysical abstraction, is a collection of dynamisms.

Responding progressively to one another within his make-up are his biological reactions, his instincts and his intellectual life, and this dynamic growth and development are never, in fact, fully completed. The important point, then, is to ensure that this individual, this person, should be progressively integrated in his free and conscious intellect, in organic and emotional impulses, in all that makes him specifically human. This formidable labor of progressive integration is never completely finished since at the end the will of the spirit to live is not great enough to preclude dying. It is in this context that the religious sentiment in man develops—in this context which is at one and the same time a growth, a call and a drama. This, too, is the background that must be taken into account, in the final analysis, not only in the religious sentiment as it subsists subjectively in mankind, but also in its orientation toward the objective reality of God and of His Word, and lifted, with the mysterious help of grace, to the transcendent level of the spiritual life in the Christian sense of this term.

Second, the emotional life is of primordial importance in this work of progressive integration, and this holds good from the very earliest years of life, even before any sort of knowledge or awareness is present. The conditioning of the higher level of the personality through the emotional life, including the unconscious, is of such immense importance that a system of education which does not take it into account must inevitably result in the failure of its purpose. The impulses, emotions and reactions which compose it, and which constitute in large measure the experiences of these early years, are *to be used* by the conscious personality, itself dynamic—that is to say, they are to be put to use in a sense that sublimates them and which is itself of a spiritual order.

Such are the viewpoints, scientifically indisputable, which will be guiding our reflections throughout the course of this work, either explicitly or implicitly. In other words, we shall endeavor to place religious education in proper relationship with the fact that man is a personal dynamism who tends, as Canon Baudoin expresses it, to pass "from instinct to spirit." To complete the expression we shall add: and to do so under the influence of grace, that is to say, of the love of God for His fallen creature.

Some readers will perhaps be surprised as they

progress through the pages that follow. They may expect to find—implicitly perhaps—the exposition of some practical rules designed to teach children to live in a Christian manner; but such a work would be pointless because it has been done already in a variety of ways. On the other hand, the ethical aspect of education, while it is important, is not the essential one. Or, at least, the ethical aspect, unless it runs the risk of ceasing to be Christian, has no meaning or effectiveness apart from spirituality. It has, therefore, seemed of greater importance to us to recall—or to emphasize—certain aspects of elementary psychology that underline precisely the necessity for the development of an authentic spiritual life if we are to arrive at a morality that can be related at one and the same time to the teaching of God and to the real nature of man. If due reflection is not given to this essential requirement a risk exists that there will result pure legalism, a doctrine remote indeed from the philosophy and the spirituality which Christ has charged the Church to bring alive in the tormented world of men.

I
The Christian Vision
of the World

RELIGIOUS education is not — in spite of the un-
doubted fact that a great many people do indeed
believe this to be its explicit function—a method for
the imparting of a standard knowledge of correct behavior. For that matter, this is not the function of
education in general. The primary role of education
is not so much to provide the child with good habits
and sound principles as to help him to take cognizance
of his human nature, and to furnish him with the
elements of knowledge and the lines along which he
may most fully discover how to adapt himself to his
condition. What constitutes the difference between
education, in the general sense of the term, and
Christian education, is that without the legacy of
divine Revelation we are very poorly equipped to
offer any reasonable explanation for the ultimate
significance and the real purpose of human life. And
so, in one sense, the matter resolves itself into the
finding of a definite dimension, a satisfying and complete synthesis, for the elements of reflection and of
the search for truth have been a part of universal
experience wherever civilization has flourished. Men
have always meditated upon good and evil, upon suffering, love and death; but when divorced from that
view of history which includes the mystery of God,
such meditations cannot lead men to any vision or
explanation that fully satisfies all questions.

To find the key to what is otherwise a mystery, we

must accept the mystery of God; that is to say, we must accept a vision that breaks through and transcends the limits of our rational knowledge, instead of obstinately confining ourselves to an unaided search and traveling around in circles that can lead to nothing other than contradiction and frustration. Primarily and essentially the religious attitude consists in this acceptance of the dialogue with the transcendent Infinity who speaks to us—in other words, the acceptance of the gift of Faith. It is an attitude to life in the fullest meaning of the term, including the field of voluntary actions, namely a moral or ethical sense. And it is just this attitude to life toward which it is of the utmost importance to direct the child.

When we say "direct" we are not speaking in the sense of to "inculcate"—a sinister word in any event —but in the sense that we should wish to provide the child with everything that will enable him to take up this attitude of his own free choice when the time shall come for him to do so. Obviously, then, it is of vital importance that the child shall not be led along bypaths away from this objective and that no one shall be given the opportunity of placing major obstacles in his way. The discovery of God is never completed, and quite often the most effective way to help a young person to find Him is to refrain from directing his search on overprecise and rigid lines, which may well result in his beginning to build his conception of God upon a caricature. It is possibly preferable not to try to "fix" too specifically certain aspects of the truth: in the final analysis it is God Himself who will make Himself known, and we know that His grace will often reach souls by quite unexpected routes. . . . It would be a very grave error if parents and educators, under the pretext of teaching the religious verities to a child should demonstrate their own lack of faith to the extent of wishing to play the role that God alone can fill.

While it is necessary, therefore, to help the child to integrate himself in a Christian concept of the world, it is perhaps not without point to call to mind essential factors in possibly slightly unusual terms and yet ones designed to convey much more clearly the educational requirements that are demanded by this Christian vision of the universe.

The Created Universe

In the light of God's teaching, what can be known of the universe appears in its entirety as an assembly of immanent forces, distinct and different, which strive, according to the design or plan of their Creator, toward the greatest fullness of being. All the elements that compose the universe need not have existed at all, but they do in fact *exist* and *in one sense only*. Just as the jets of water in a fountain spurt from tier to tier ever higher and higher, so all the elements of the universe leap forth from nothingness, rising to levels more or less developed until they reach man, conscious and free, who sums them all up and responds in their name, and in the light of his thinking soul, to the question of God.

Matter that is inert, that is, as the term connotes, without the inherent power of moving, subsists in its form without, however, participating in its own life. The uniqueness of the individual pebble is the result of a certain number of physical laws and accidental occurrences, but the pebble itself has no power to shape the course of its development nor is it required to maintain its form by its own energies. Whatever may be held about the composition of nature in terms of energy, the fact remains that if a material thing or being is as it is, there is a reason for it, and individualization at this point is dependent upon other factors and merely a matter of classification.

We next come to the first and unheralded movement of vegetative life. A vegetable, whether single or multicellular, is still composed of matter, but it also possesses an absolutely new kind of energy—a life force that consists in the vegetable subsisting by itself. The vegetable is a mass of matter that holds together of its own accord and in its own unique form; it draws from around itself that which is necessary for its existence; it rejects all that has become incompatible with its continued existence. Each individual vegetable—and this is the primordial characteristic of every living being—is endowed with this overwhelming power to be itself, to maintain its individual existence, to be with, one might almost say, intense tenacity its unique self, which may be compared with other things but is never absorbed in them.

This astonishing power is to be found in the most minute form of seaweed, in the most majestic cedars of the forests, in the most unobtrusive flower of the countryside. Moreover, the living organism, the lowest stage of which is this vegetable life, possesses the power to continue, within the unity of this very same specific form, its survival by the system of reproduction, sexual or otherwise. Not the least wonderful aspect of this phenomenon occurs to us when we reflect that one grain of seed contains sufficient energy to raise by its own power a new individual plant of its own species. In a word, at this stage we may say of vegetal life that to live is to possess the power to accumulate and to maintain the material necessary to its own organic life and its own unique existence, which means also the power to maintain that uniqueness in the face of the wear and tear of time. Already, then, we have encountered an immanent energy, a dynamism, autonomous and hidden, that strains toward stable existence.

These same characteristics appear at the level of animal life. But here we meet a novel modification that could be described as a perfection of or an advance upon this already existing autonomy, in so far as the living animal is, in addition, endowed with the power of feeling, that is to say, but in a sense as yet very primitive, of the power of knowing. No matter how rudimentary this sense may be, the fact remains that there is here something new: a sensory and nervous system, distinct, finely wrought and functionally operative. This new organic structure is what comprises the animal's power to move, what distinguishes animal life from that of vegetal tropism in that it is a power which is not the result of a chemical reaction or attraction, but is a very complex performance of responses given through the nerve centers to sense impressions willingly or knowingly perceived: the cat hears, sees, "senses" mice—these impressions are synthesized in a coherent ensemble whose perception by the animal releases his activity.

All of this is to be found in man, who is an animal. But when we reach this level everything changes in such a completely radical manner that it is extremely difficult to express or formulate at the same time clearly and with sufficient force what has happened. This change is the transcendent phenomenon of self-consciousness: the animal (man) is no longer an animal any more than a vegetable; he stands at a level of autonomy that cannot be compared with what has preceded him; he knows that he knows; he knows himself as a part of his knowledge; he verifies his knowledge, he thinks, he reasons, he reflects. He is the celebrated "thinking reed" of Pascal. He thinks, he reasons, and he reflects, often quite wrongly; but that has nothing at all to do with the outstanding fact that he does reflect.

Even as sense knowledge in the animal produces as a consequence movement properly so called, so in man his knowledge, conscious and rational, produces the ultimate in autonomy; in other words, liberty— the need for every human individual *himself* to participate in his own destiny. It is an extraordinarily difficult undertaking to speak of liberty. And yet it is of the most intense interest, since education in the final analysis consists essentially in the cultivation and the promotion of the liberty of the future adults.

The clearest way, perhaps, lies through a comparison between the dynamisms of activity in the animal and in man. In the light of this comparison, liberty will appear as a kind of negative, as an instinct insufficiently effective for leading the human being to the destiny suited to his human condition. For there remains a margin of error which the human subject *alone* can personally correct and complete, precisely because of the fact that he has knowledge of himself, and that he can make his own decisions according to this knowledge, and according to the crude forces of his instinctive impulses. He can even grasp the fact— and much more often than is commonly believed—that his knowledge may be in direct contradiction to the instinctive impulses which, however, he cannot master; that is to say that he cannot fully succeed in following a course of behavior which he has nevertheless chosen and *determined* to follow. We might say that, in one sense, herein is where human suffering lies. The contradiction intrinsic in this situation is the direct proof of the existence of human liberty.

Modern psychology assists us in fixing the causes —in the medical sense of the word—of this situation, sometimes even in partially neutralizing them, either by preventive methods in the course of education, or by curative methods in the course of psychotherapy. And even if a system of education that ideally allows for the real growth of the human being never wholly succeeds in the perfect achievement of its aims, it would still undoubtedly limit the amount of damage that is often done otherwise, and would so much the better prepare individuals for the fulfillment of their several destinies.

The created universe appears then as an organic ensemble progressively elaborated according to the creative design of God, whose complex forces of energy culminate at the level of mankind. The result, at this level, is man's full participation in an existence conscious of itself, in a certain sense responsible to itself, an existence, moreover, which has become not secondary or transitory but primordial and free from conceivable or acceptable destruction. To speak of participation in existence is now to say participation in God Himself, since the name of God, unveiled to Moses, is the first person of the verb "to be" in Hebrew.

But the dynamism of man did not and does not reach its fruition in time. It is fraught with something which contradicts it, which curbs it and which indeed tends to disrupt it. The conscience and free will of the man do not completely succeed in disengaging him from the animal or the vegetable condition. These two primitive states are not totally assimilated, illumined or transfigured by the power of the spirit. That is shown on the vegetative plane by the persistence of the biological mechanisms that escape the conscious will, and by the fact that the "human material" does not succeed in overcoming biological old age or the corruptibility of living matter which is completed by death. On the sensory and animal plane it is manifested by the persistence of a psychic zone that is never wholly penetrated by the light of the conscious mind, in other words by the permanent existence, more or less turbulent, of an emotional substratum of which the discernible psychological life is unaware. This is precisely the world that is being explored by modern psychology; it is just such knowledge and the use to which we can put such knowledge that are indispensable to the proper understanding of human behavior and its significance.

The inevitable discovery of this fact is the very source of human anguish in all its forms and does not allow of explanation according to the measure of our reasoning. It is too vast, too universal, too "cosmic" and too fundamental for us to grasp fully all its co-ordinating elements. In other words, it escapes the limits of knowledge and bypasses them. God alone can lift the veil and give us the gleams of light that allow us to catch a glimpse of the truth that is within the grasp of all of us.

This is the story of Genesis, a truly historical one under its popular form, the point of departure of all the progressive action of God in the history of man. The intoxication of conscious liberty unbalanced man and filled him with an illusion of all-powerfulness, so that he forgot that he was only a relative being, entirely ruled by and entirely dependent upon the love of his Creator. This was the first stage. Through this sin of pride, temporal life and the human spirit suffered permanent impairment, and man was forced to realize that he was incapable despite the illusion of his power of completely fulfilling his own destiny. Yet the love of God is still more transcendent, if one may so express it, than was imagined even beneath the tents of Exodus. The struggle was not over, and in a certain sense it was absolutely indispensable for man to perceive in his own consciousness and with almost intolerable intensity the insufficiency of a temporal destiny. God wanted more for him than that. Then, as the thoughts of His children matured, God inscribed His name for them through His Incarnate Word, and takes it upon Himself to send Him again in sovereign glory to bring the world of time to a close. On a certain spring day, in the year thirty of our era, He died, and He rose again from the dead, thus demonstrating the supreme victory of Love and giving to all the human race and to each living individual personally the answer to his tribulation and the fulfillment of his own driving energy.

This, in brief, is the vision of the world, previously chaotic, which has assumed its own positive rhythm and its total fullness through the real presence of God in its history.

This is the existential vision which the man of tomorrow, virtually walking around in the child of today, needs in order to be fully himself. And it is to give him access to it that religious education properly so called should be molded, with the infinite respect due to this free individual whom God calls to an intimate knowledge of Himself.

To allow the child to ascertain and the man to plumb the consciousness of his vocation and of his place in the living universe, this, in fine, is the purpose and end of religious education. The point is to aid each person at the beginning of his pilgrimage to find his place in this immense dynamism, impaired but now redeemed by Infinite Love, according to the working out of "God's Plan" as we might say; to help him to achieve the full realization of this extraordinary gift, quite beyond our conception, of true life totally luminous and lasting which breaks free from the limitations of the temporal.

Outside of this concept of the whole there can be only distortion, regressions and bitterness; in other words, betrayal of this dramatic colloquy which has been commenced between Humanity and its Creator who saves it and establishes its eternal existence in His dominion.

II
Love
and
Narcissism

IF the primary significance of the energy of the universe is a straining toward existence (to such an extent that at the level of consciousness death is regarded as a bitter defeat), its secondary significance is a straining, almost equally as imperative, toward the greatest and the most enduring unity in the relationships of human beings, one with another, or, in other words, toward the establishment of an actual, tangible communion with other people. There is nothing here, of course, that will surprise the Christian; he knows that God, the ineffable and Most Holy Trinity, is perfect communion in Himself, and that human nature is made in the likeness of God.

There is no necessity to go into detail as to all the various manifestations of this longing for unity. On the professional plane, in the world of sport, in local affairs, in matters of national importance, and even, yes, even in international affairs, the urge toward unity and peace is one of the most fundamental in the human make-up. It culminates in intensity through the sexual instinct, that is to say, through this force of love at the level of the sense perceptions and of the emotions expressing in such an extraordinarily intense way the profound and universal need for love and for companionship which is the fundamental constituent of human nature.

There is no need, either, to underline and expand upon the subject of how this deep-seated urge toward unity is contradicted in practice, and even endangered to the point of failure, total or partial.

Here again depth psychology shows us what happens—and gives valuable aid within a limited scope on how to remedy it—but Christian Revelation alone gives us the key to the mystery. At least we can attempt to express it in terms of Christian Revelation, but in fact this key is itself a mystery which far surpasses in its magnitude the limited power of our reasoning.

The study of the psycho-affective evolution of the human being shows very well both the origin of the constraint that interposes itself in opposition to the complete establishment of a total and general intercourse with others and its true character.

Formation of the "Ego"

The conscious personality—let us call it the "ego" —is slow in forming because it is slow in breaking away from the emotional and instinctual mists of infancy and very early childhood. Its formation appears as a progressive and difficult adaptation to needs that become more and more elaborate and further and further involved in relationships with others. From the newborn baby to the adult of twenty-five years of age there takes place a progression from total dependence on others for life and life's needs to total participation of these with others —or at least for everything to proceed smoothly along the lines which the study of this evolution suggests, there *should* be this progression. In the progressive acquisition of his autonomy, which is his constitutional necessity, the thinking human being should acquire, at the same time and in the same proportion, the feeling for spontaneous self-sacrifice that would help him to participate more and more in communion with the rest of the human race, and make him correspondingly less dependent upon it at all the different levels on which human life is actually lived. Without being in the least paradoxical one might say that the human being is less autonomous to the degree that he falls short of self-discipline for or adjustment to the community. Anyone who has a *need of others* to acquire a feeling of security or fulfillment shows thereby that he has retained the emotional attitude of early childhood; anyone who cannot rely on or trust in his own resources, as Rilke says—we would say, try out his own unique personality—is in direct proportion dependent, or lacking in autonomy. The ideal normal adult man would be he who fully, spontaneously and positively felt the need not *of* others but *to be with others* and *to be something to others*.

But the ideal adult normal man does not exist. Every personality tends toward this ideal, more or less; but no one completely succeeds in attaining it precisely because of the constraint already referred to which intervenes during the course of the emotional evolution from childhood.

This evolution is made by stages (we shall return to this theory later) perfectly clear and distinct, although the chronological developments that separate them allow for an important margin of uncertainty. The fact is that the human being in childhood passes from adaptation to a primary state of need to positive and progressive adaptation to a secondary state of need; and this occurs at several different times during the first years of his life.

This transition is particularly significant at the moment of birth. In the life of the womb the child, totally passive and secure from the world outside, finds his biological needs entirely satisfied by means of his mother, without having to take any of the initiative in procuring them. Then, suddenly, he is expelled from the womb: that is to say, he is abruptly required to adapt himself to this quite new state of existence, more in conformity with his true nature, undoubtedly, because it is more autonomous, but in which, in order to go on living, he now has to take the initiative in breathing, seeing that he is kept sufficiently warm and in sucking to obtain nourishment.

If we dwell seriously upon this for a short while we shall realize that this upheaval, for such in the strongest sense it is, is both considerable and dramatic. Certainly the psychic life of the newborn baby is at least obscure and chaotic; but it does exist, although this could only be on the most elementary emotional plane. Already, however, there is this to be noted, that the transition assures to the child the first demands of his autonomy: to be, and to be *himself*, however confusedly and instinctively at first, it is necessary for him to pay attention to the exterior world, for him to "offer himself" to it, so to speak, and to become part of it.

The same process of transition takes place, for example, and in a comparable way, at the time of weaning. Now the child, previously exclusively dependent on his mother from the point of view of nourishment (and, for that matter, for all his sensory satisfaction), moves out to a certain extent from this dependence and acquires a slightly more palpable degree of autonomy and of initiative which will help him in enlarging the field of his activities and of his relationships with others.

Then, by various stages to which we shall be returning in due course, this will develop into a progressive hold upon autonomy by means of harmonious intercourse with others in the parental and family circles. At every stage of development the emotional personality of the child is torn, in a way, between two profound forces: the extent of the need which manifests itself, and which impels, and adherence to the preceding situation already tried and found relatively satisfying. At every stage the situation next to come shows itself to be both richer from the point of view of the opening up and extending of relationships, and vaguely disturbing by reason of its new and untried character. This sort of dilemma, at certain times very acute, is conquered in the early years on the purely emotional plane, and not by reason or reflection. It is only when he reaches the drama of his adolescence that the young person very confusedly attains to this characteristic condition of the human being.

It is, of course, easy to understand that in the course of these successive changes the necessary evolution cannot always be fully achieved without shocks. What is more, it is impossible to predict how such and such a newborn baby will get over his first adaptation to emerging from the womb, or how he will react to weaning. In ideal theory the child should come successfully through stage A of his needs so as to arrive positively and with no curb on his progressive dynamism at stage B. In other words, he should be emotionally capable of relinquishing the need of A.

If he has not been properly satisfied at stage A, the necessary and inevitable transition to stage B will carry with it a certain tinge of nostalgia, if one may put it that way; in other words, the emotional dynamism will remain cramped; will rest, as it were, upon a void, upon a sense of dissatisfaction which life, unrolling day after day, will make more and more obscure and insoluble. This is the kind of thing one observes in adults handicapped in their psychological development through an *unconscious* and unattainable quest for some such lack from which they suffered at the age of somewhere between six months and two to five years. The situation, which is known psychologically as the narcissistic regression is universal—that is to say, no human being can escape it *completely*. As a matter of cold fact, however, it is inevitable if a child has been frequently the victim of such disappointments and frustrations between its birth and the age of about eight years. Most of the time the ill effects will show later on in such slight traits or reflexes as will be deemed oddities, eccentricities and whims. Where the damage has been grave, however—as, for example, in a family environment that is disunited and unhappy—the risks of neuroses properly so called are evidently greater.

The same process of narcissistic regression or fixation can make its appearance, through an apparent paradox, if stage A is too prolonged and its needs satisfied beyond their time. The child must be assisted in achieving the transition, his task must be made easier, and he must be sustained in his efforts at relinquishment and transcendence which are essential to his progressive adaptation to the ensuing stages. In this matter the example of weaning is perhaps the most obvious. The longer his primitive state of satisfaction is retained, that is to say, the longer the child is kept dependent upon the maternal milk or on bottle-feeding, the greater will be the frustration he experiences at the time weaning begins; the more difficult will it be for him to overcome to the point of forgetting, of relegating to the plane of unconscious reflexes, his primitive way of wanting satisfaction. It is a clinical fact, well known to experts, that weanings which are delayed too long are very often the generators of emotional "twists" of the narcissistic type and even of neuroses.

One does not overstate the case to say that the later normal development of the child's life in relation to others, emotional at first and rational afterward, can be partially dependent on a weaning achieved more or less correctly at about six months of age and in a properly flexible and progressive manner.

The psychological effects of correct or incorrect weaning which we have outlined are applicable in their implications for all the ensuing stages of emotional development which we shall be touching upon in the course of this work. As of now, however, it is essential that our readers should keep in mind the central importance of the constant and fatal risk of narcissistic regression in the child. In fact, the first emotional reactions registered in the instinctive psychology of the first years of life will never be completely forgotten or obliterated. And the narcissistic regression in all its forms may constitute a serious hindrance or even a positive obstacle to the development of an authentic religious life. This latter, in the Christian view, is essentially characterized by a progressive, though as we know never fully achieved, renewal of a spirit of sacrifice and openness of heart, in the Pascalian sense, growing ever fuller and richer as life proceeds. In other words the religious life is a continuation of the relinquishment and dynamic transcendence that allows the soul to attain through the grace of God and in the light of faith (an attitude of course supra-emotional or rational) to the true community of spirit, and, as it is expressed in theological language, to perfect charity.

It is very clear that this religious life has all the greater chance of successful establishment and growth right from the start if the first emotional stages are achieved with the minimum of "twists" or narcissistic regressions. To the measure that these latter appear they throw the person back upon emotional preoccupations that are strictly egocentric. It is not a question of returning to the past in general, but to one's own special feeling of dissatisfaction, exclusive of the rest of the world. The exclusion of "the other" as a *subject,* the resentment against "the other" for some satisfaction not granted, all this lives on in the personality in the form of *unconscious* re-flexes. This expresses an attitude directly opposed to normal growth and maturity on the one hand and to supernatural expansion under the action of grace on the other.

These particular psychological considerations, founded upon clinical research and the observation of facts, are indeed pregnant with significance. They pose the all-important problem of the contradiction between the world of reality and the heart of man. They cannot be ignored, for their findings all aid the child in facing precisely this problem and in opening his ears to the answer of God.

It is striking to remark that Revelation itself starts with this fact of the narcissistic regression. In the first pages of the Bible this springs to the attention in a surprising way. In the story of the creation of man and woman, Adam recognizes in Eve "bone of my bones, and flesh of my flesh"; that is why man "shall leave father and mother, and shall cleave to his wife; and they shall be two in one flesh." Yet immediately after the Fall, to Jehovah's question Adam replied: *"The woman* whom *thou* gavest me . . ." Thus the couple were separated, disunity was introduced; the wonderful union between two people was disrupted. At the heart of the human person this rupture still persists profoundly: the longing for unity in love and the constant relapse into the prison of the individual. It was necessary for God Himself to come in person to re-establish the victorious unity in a gesture of Infinite Love achieved by His Incarnation in human history and in human form.

Such is, in fact, the ultimate point of departure of all education which is to be looked upon as religious: true *existence* or *being* is not possible except in the measure in which one exists in unity with the rest of mankind; but the inevitable constraint of the narcissistic regression engraved so obscurely in our psychological life hinders us until death which therefore becomes the sole means of achieving full life.

Psychological Research and Revelation

While psychology can describe the process of narcissism and, in theory at least, can discern its origins, it can do no more than recognize a certain condition to be found in human nature that is normal insofar as it is universal. Psychopathology can intervene to assist this condition only if the regressions are actually neurotic, namely if occasionally or habitually they impair the facility of the individual in question to adapt himself to reality. But this normal universal fact or condition, which in truth is the source of all human suffering, paradoxically makes its appearance as a contradiction or a failure. If there were no instinctive tendency in man to revert to the past, if he had none of these reflexes of the narcissistic regression, there would be no strife, no misunderstandings, no unhappiness, no troubles. There would be no evil and no suffering.

Revelation in its turn throws light upon this human state of affairs of which psychological research and learning can give us only a descriptive survey touching upon its mechanisms and its effects. That is the idea, so often evoked but so seldom explained, of "concupiscence." At the very origin of human nature there is the unbalance arising from the heady intoxication of the knowledge of liberty which caused the created being to lose the sense of his relative position to his Creator. This is the whole mystery of original sin: human nature breaks its relationship with God and presumes to arrange its own destiny. In other words, human nature becomes set, as it were, on the quest for a state of being which it knows by experience, but which is far below the state desired for it by God. It limits itself to the lure of certain values that are substantial and satisfying only insofar as they are clearly recognized as transitory, relative, incomplete, or unattainable by human power alone. The desires of human nature are contrary to its true dynamism and its real destiny. Yet the dynamism in itself is both good and properly oriented: it is the dynamism of love, notwithstanding the fact that it is divided and inconsistent, and incapable of freeing itself completely from its restraints. There, in fact, lies the profound split so strongly emphasized by St. Paul, over and over again, but principally in Chapter VII of the Epistle to the Romans. Despite all our love of the good, that is, of God and of communion with God, something within ourselves still tries to restrain our striving toward Him. We cannot harmoniously or easily fit ourselves into the vital and reciprocal rhythm of the universe as constituted by the Creator. In a world of totally interchanging relationships we have become isolated units, thrown back upon the chimerical and egocentric desire to be absolutes in ourselves, and we remain paralyzed on the road of life.

The child bears this fundamental handicap within him. While he is liberated from it to a certain extent by baptism because of his accession to membership in the Mystical Body of Christ, he will not get rid of it during the course of his temporal existence. That is to say, he is still the bearer of this "contra-dynamism" of concupiscence which causes him to look for evil contrary to his very will, as St. Paul says.

It should be remembered that the parents and the educators of the child are themselves burdened by this same handicap of human nature. What they have is some personal experience of the struggle, of the failures and of the renewed efforts. They have therefore, been able—at least in theory—to acquire a certain knowledge of themselves and of the human enigma, and of the necessity to cling both in their anxiety and their hope to the person of Christ from whom comes salvation. This much they could transmit; or, more exactly, it is toward this that they could assist the children under their guidance to aspire personally, each one in the mystery of his own incommunicable autonomy.

If psychologically and theologically speaking, education is before all a "work of guidance," it must inevitably, whenever this becomes necessary, do the work of correcting. But it is imperative that educators should know how to avoid both the excesses of foolish optimism and those of hidebound pessimism, and to know this as much from the point of view of psychology as from the spiritual point of view.

For the moment let us leave on one side the problems posed by the emotional personality of the parents or the educators; we shall return to this later. We shall here consider only the child and his potentialities which require to be developed. If the educator starts from a systematically pessimistic conception he can proceed only to the thwarting *a priori* of all the child's inclinations and aspirations. If these are presupposed to be wholly bad, obviously rigid and principally negative boundaries will be replaced on all the child's energies. The child will, of course, get the impression that he has been always wrong, and that all his desires have been crooked from their very source. He will then have to live according to an artificial rule which not only fails to attract him but in fact causes him to suffer continually.

The resultant psychological state is quite clear: the child who is being constantly frustrated in his normal desires and requirements can but accumulate instinctive regressions of the narcissistic type; he will be driven constantly back upon his hunger for fulfillment and his unhappiness, and will inevitably close in upon himself. His normal aggressiveness, being continuously suppressed, will have the tendency to store up a kind of smoldering energy that will burst forth someday in a spectacular and very likely quite reckless revolt; or alternatively, he will turn in upon himself in a complete neurosis of failure and frustration. With regard to the spiritual result, it will go exactly the same way: the more he advances the more the child becomes inaccessible to love, to gentleness, to self-sacrifice; the older he grows the more God appears to him in the monstrous guise of a vigilant policeman; he will either submit passively or else he will knock down this hideous idol with one blow. His quest for religion will be ruined for many a long day, and it will take all the mysterious power of grace, and possibly many dramatic happenings, to introduce a little bit of true light into this night without hope.

If, on the other hand, we start from the conception of blind optimism—along the lines somewhat of Jean Jacques Rousseau—the child will be left to pursue his own way, encouraged in all his experiments, without any clear or enlightened direction, and will wallow in his own primitive incoherence. He will not learn to make allowances for or adjustments to a real world outside of himself, still less to consider the personalities of other people who are pursuing their own legitimate aims. He will not be able to draw anything from his own emotional experience that will enable him to expand normally in conscious relations with others in the very real world in which he lives. Psychologically there is a very grave risk of inducing in such a child a narcissistic regression quite as strong as that brought upon the child educated on opposite lines. The world of reality—the world of material things, the animal or human world—will inevitably resist and oppose the impulses of this child. This will be to him a source of fatal frustration. And as his educational climate has not prepared him, but rather the opposite, to treat frustrations as a part of the experience necessary for a positive adaptation to life, the reaction of the egocentric recoil is intense. The spoiled child is never happy; he lacks something all the time, and he does not know what it is. The very expression itself is most apt: he is "spoiled" even before he can mature, and life will hold for him a continual taste for contradiction that is at times intolerable. In his defensive reaction to this state of affairs he himself will quite readily become intolerable in his own turn, arousing in others aggressive reflexes which serve to complicate the whole situation indefinitely. With regard to the spiritual result . . . If God, in the course of this child's existence, does not give him immediate satisfaction for anything he requires, of what use is God? And yet this is an added unhappiness; the suffering which he cannot assume engenders, in a sort of diabolical, vicious circle, "the suffering of having to suffer." The religious horizon is closed down, since everything in the whole world is resented according to the egocentric pattern of this mind. The "spoiled" child can never give his life in order to find it according to the evangelical outlook. And so the night falls here, too, and without hope.

Erroneous Demands of Educators

For the educator the most difficult undertaking undoubtedly consists in striving to form for oneself the most complete picture possible of the interior world of the child, without, naturally, projecting into it one's own interior outlook. This, however, is the supreme necessity. Since education amounts in actual fact to befriending, guiding, correcting, and coordinating the autonomy of the child, his initiative and his endeavors, so must one realize to the full all that he is capable of at any given moment of his evolution and development. Many of the educational errors arise, it would seem, from educators demanding things from children without fully realizing that these are beyond their powers. Such demands can but increase to an excessive degree the unhappiness normally inevitable at each stage of development. And in the measure in which this distress is excessive, the possibility of an adaptation to ensuing situations is paralyzed, or at the least partially so.

An athlete at the start of his career does not begin by lifting a hundredweight bar bell. Even supposing that he could do so, the effort would be so exhausting for such a small result that he would quickly give up the sport, unless he were so obsessed that in the violence of his energy he had to give up anyway through bringing about some accident to his muscular power of movement. He will begin with ten-pound weights, and he will so gradually and progressively increase the power of his performance that he will hardly be aware of it himself when one day he will lift the hundredweight with ease. The comparison is quite classic; and contemporary psychology has brought nothing new to it, unless it be to highlight more strongly the sound accuracy of this point.

But let it be noted that the athlete at the outset of his course of training *knows* that he *wants* to reach the power of lifting that one hundredweight bar bell.

How many parents are capable—in educational matters as they are in others—of encouraging their children genuinely, with patience and complete disinterestedness, instead of the more obviously easy course of demand and punishment?

At the extreme, this kind of educational "boosting" can lead to the growth of an attitude that wants to throw up the whole thing—like the athlete and the weights. This corresponds to that code of false morality which our late Holy Father condemned on many different occasions. It turns upon a theory that arises from confused thinking. From the fact that a certain person, in a certain actual situation, is perhaps not yet altogether capable of avoiding a certain fault, it is deduced quite falsely that he is not *bound* by objective and universal moral rules. From such a proof of failure it is then assumed that this is an indication of the standards attainable by him. This is narcissism again, in the sense that, to fly from a conflict and from a necessary sacrifice, one gives to a particular subjective course of behavior a general character it does not possess. The moral ideal which the Law describes, the absolute standard value, does not depend upon individual variations from it. In fact, of course, a standard has been relinquished, but this is camouflaged by a pride that does not wish to recognize the weakness.

From our position, according to which Christian education should help its subject to develop to the best of his positive and relational potentialities, such an accepted stagnation just will not do. All human life and behavior, let us not forget, takes place in a dialogue between people in a world of relationships: of human beings with each other and of man with God.

If the child has a deep-felt need not to be crushed by anxiety and culpability, he has equally the need to be stimulated and encouraged, to discover progressively all the demands of his situation as a man and as a son of God; to consider them as his own, and to know himself in relation to them since he is personally and entirely committed to his situation. Moral education organized around the idea of fault and punishment will not help him. But a moral education centered upon the demands of good and on the *virtues* in the most positive sense will permit him not to be swallowed up in an egocentric evaluation of his culpability in some passing situation, which involves a secondary problem only. The faults—which are inevitable—that he will commit will help him, instead, to know his weaknesses better. This is certainly so, but what is more, they will help him to know, by contrast, the resources in himself or the problems in his relations with others that he had only dimly apprehended. At the same time they will give him the profound experience of human weakness no longer plunged in a stifling bitterness but in the hope of the Redemption. It is in this sense that St. Augustine dwells upon the apparent paradox of the usefulness of sin.

These few reflections upon the dialectic of optimism and of pessimism, and of the error manifested by the false morality of which we have been speaking, cannot find a better conclusion than in this enlightening text of the Council of Trent:

"God does not ordain that we do the impossible; but in giving His commandments He enjoins us to do what we can and to demand that which we cannot" (Council of Trent, session IV, Chapter XI. Denz. 804).

III

Examination of the "Unconscious" of Parents

IT IS a commonplace frequently and rightly stated that the family environment is of particular importance in the matter of education in general and of religious education in particular. But this primary truth should not be interpreted solely in its customary sense of a psychological and spiritual environment consciously experienced.

On the contrary, attention should be drawn to the unconscious conditionings of the emotional life in the child—conditionings which are, for one thing, the psychological content with which he has been endowed and to which a valid religious orientation can ultimately be given. No one can seriously dispute the well-established and well-known fact that the first seven or eight years in the life of the human being, with all they contain of emotions, reactions, emotional intensity, are primordial in that they provide the ground plan, as it were, for the whole personality. Not that they constitute it. There is, in fact, the congenital raw material upon which heredity undoubtedly comes into play in a very considerable way and yet in a way that evades precise evaluation. This is the potential material which will be shaped, oriented and in various ways stabilized by the emotional experiences of the first years of life and what will remain of those experiences beneath the level of the conscious memory.

Now it should not be forgotten that every human being possesses an unconscious; in other terms he has been a child himself and not all the emotional experiences of his own childhood have been totally "liquidated," according to the technical expression. This means that the parents, the people primarily charged with the work of education—and above all with the forming of the bases upon which it can be built—themselves possess an emotional unconscious. It is impossible that this unconscious should not provoke in parents certain attitudes or reactions that have nothing at all to do with their decisions or rational choices, but which would have all the more effect upon the emotions of the child in that these parents are hardly aware of the existence of the unconscious and therefore are not in a position to direct it, to use it, or even to curb it.

One pathological example will be much easier to understand than a lengthy theoretical exposition. It often happens that a young man who shows signs of scrupulosity anxiety, makes a reference to the fact that his father, or mother, showed similar signs. A careful psychotherapeutic treatment will succeed, in a great number of such cases, in eliminating the troubles of the son. Here it is a matter of something that is part of such a person's make-up. But mention may also be made of a condition that is not so much the result of heredity as of a kind of "contagion" picked up in the parental environment. The scrupulosity anxiety of the parent, even if he is aware of it and tries to restrain it, is translated into a profound sentiment of insecurity with regard to himself and has, therefore, strong chances of provoking the same sensation of insecurity, confused perhaps but intense, in the child, even a small child, if he or she is particularly sensitive, or if, as sometimes happens certain circumstances have made him sensitive, though he may be the only one thus affected in a whole family of children.

Yet the parents who read these pages should be

reassured on this point. The example given is pathological and such disorders do not take place quite as
simply as might appear from a description of them.
The modern psychology of dynamisms, while it
obliges parents to consider each child in the light of
his own personal history, induces them also to consider him in the light of the mystery of his individuality—literally in that very area of his mind which
cannot be explored by psychology, in the indetermi-
nate and unascertainable area of his personality.
Moreover, the history of each person is, in fact, a
dialogue, or rather a kind of dialogue between the
mystery of God and the mystery of this person. This
escapes all investigation and therefore all mathematical forecasting. It is not because grace is not a fact
of experimental science in itself that it should for
that reason be overlooked when facing the various
problems of education. The parents do whatever
they can and all they can, but their field of action
is nevertheless limited. If they do the best they can
there is no necessity for them to retain any sense of
distress or self-reproach in the event of failure,
whether serious or not; there is nothing more to do
and they can only, while regretting any errors, put
their hand into God's and allow Him to act.

The proper attitude and solution to the matter is,
of course, for parents to apprehend the relative nature of their position. That means, if one may use
this paradoxical expression, that they should be conscious of the unconscious, and should accept what
flows from the recognition of this.

"The examination of the unconscious" in the
matter of education is perhaps a more necessary
operation than the examination of the conscience
which is the conscious. How many contradictions are
there, so often unperceived, between the excellent
educational intentions and the thousand reflexes, attitudes and emotional reactions that make up the

actual daily life of these complex personalities who are coupled together and commonly designated under the oversimplified term of "parents"!

However, once again it is essential that this "examination of the unconscious" should be made calmly; we would even say in *peace* in the sense in which Christ used the term in the Gospel of St. John. The objection that rises to the lips of the "parents" is always the same: "But surely this would mean that we should be absolutely perfect, detached, calm, complete masters of ourselves, practically angels or saints!" Yes, certainly, it would mean that for them, just as it means it for everyone else in all walks of life. . . . Only no one ever attains to such perfection as that. People can only strive toward it, without losing their heads when they realize that no one has ever completely succeeded in reaching it. The parents, as we have already said, have been children themselves, that is to say, they, too, had parents. These parents had parents in their turn, and so on. In this unbroken and unending chain, which goes back right to the mystery of the original contradiction, there has been only one human person, historically, who has attained this complete psychological balance: Mary, Mother of Christ, who has expressed, on the plane of daily life, God's intention in respect of her.

In this changing and varied world of modern "personal" psychology there can be no question of describing or classifying all the facts and all the situations which arise. It would be impossible and confusing to give a theoretical list of all the unconscious phenomena possible among parents and the repercussions thereof upon the evolution of their children.

However, some large general problems can be mentioned as examples in order to draw the attention of readers to the daily reality of these facts, which are all the more important in that for the most part they are quite misunderstood.

The Possessive Instinct

Without any doubt the most important of these unconscious emotional problems is the possessive instinct. There is no question here, of course, of dealing with the pathological and unnatural cases which everyone knows exist, and which are, therefore, clearly in evidence by reason of their very excesses. We shall deal simply with the persistent reflexes of an emotional attitude that is at once possessive and egocentric and that is to be found in every normal human being who has been incompletely fulfilled in the course of his evolution, and which is a corollary of this mystery of disintegration which is called original sin. Most of the time these are the reflexes which no one really evaluates and which go against the deliberate orientations provided by education. They can be expressed sometimes by explicit acts or words, but most frequently they will show themselves by a thousand imponderables, by almost imperceptible and yet repetitive signs. The emotional life of the child is particularly responsive to them precisely because he cannot subtract from them the emotional power with which his parents express or he recognizes them. There are many very possessive ways of showing one's affection for a child even by saying "Good morning" to him. . . .

The possessive reactions in regard to human beings whoever they are simply show the persistence of an emotional condition in the person concerned that would be normal in a child but in this case have not been properly outgrown. Such reactions consist in this, that, despite the most deliberate intentions of treating the other person as a subject, there still instinctively persists the "feeling" for him as an object, i.e. the feeling for him as something over which one may exercise one's influence of power or from which one may demand a certain amount of satisfaction. Yet the child is a human being, even if, as with an infant of a week old, his human quality is still hidden in the chaos of his elementary experiences of life. Whatever his age may be, the child is already a subject, and should be thus integrally considered. Otherwise, much later, having been frustrated in the experience of this most salutary sensation, he will instinctively in his turn have the tendency to treat others as objects.

There is here a sort of vicious circle whose existence, even though it is not fatal, should be clearly appreciated by those who undertake the task of educating others. Nothing is easier than, without realizing it, to take a child for an object: generally speaking, the child will take a certain length of time to put up a resistance. How many of the adolescent conflicts have their origins in such circumstances? The primary necessity for people undertaking the role of parents is obviously to get it thoroughly into their minds that the children are not their "personal property" so to speak. But rather that they are responsible to these *individuals*, which their children already are, and to God. Furthermore, this responsibility is only relative; and it matters greatly that the parents should begin by accepting the idea that they could make mistakes, despite their best wishes, that it is impossible, indeed, that they should not be sometimes wrong, and that, when all is said and done, the mystery of grace will be playing its part in the situation.

The persistence, or the recurrences, of an egocentric possessive instinct can be found, for example, in the father, if he is inclined to take up certain authoritarian attitudes of the "paterfamilias" type. Such a man would be one who, in his own childhood, had suffered vaguely from a sense of belittlement, and he will retain much later on a very deep-rooted tendency to compensate for this feeling, which, having been neither resolved nor appeased, still persists in his emotional unconscious. A dozen diverse circumstances may have provoked the awakening of this primitive emotion, and once again, not necessarily in any neurotic or unhealthy way, but to the extent of its being as it were a point of oscillation, the generator of a "defect of character."

The classic example is that of the child of two or three years who gets the impression, without there being any positive fault on the part of the people around him, that he has lost his former importance on account of the birth of another baby. A certain unconscious fear can remain from this, corresponding more or less to the condition described in current parlance, possibly wrongly, as an "inferiority complex." When he himself becomes a man and the father of a family, he still carries, though without being aware of it, this fundamental fear, and he will be acutely sensitive to anything that reminds him that he is only relative after all; his tendency will be instinctively to react against this by asserting his personality too strongly, and his reaction will be all the more intense because the fear being unconscious will be all the more acute. We have all heard of the "timid souls" who in their family circle recover the sense of indisputable authority that they can never obtain elsewhere, forgetting, in spite of themselves, that no human being is fit to wield an indisputable authority. . . . The opposite is also commonly seen: the typical "worm" of popular comedy who trembles before his wife, his mother-in-law or his children, and plays the complete bully when he is his office with his staff. But that, too, because it means that he is running away from his proper role of father and guide, will bring reactions of frustration. . . .

Generally speaking, maternal possessiveness is a little different from this. To begin with, the mother does not wear the mask of authority to such an extent, unless, on the plane of character the mother is the man of the family. Most frequently it is the persistence of a desire to coddle her family. Quite often this arises from a lack of fulfillment as a wife, whether as the result of some personal blockage or arising from difficulties in her conjugal life. Nothing is so disquieting as these women, unfortunately far too numerous, who declare, not without a certain pride that reveals the presence of unconscious conflicts to the experienced observer: "Of course I am much more of a mother than a wife. . . ." That could be translated as follows: "Not being able to achieve falling in love, I fall back upon my children so as to have something to love."

But these people regard their children in such a light that it is intolerable to them to watch them grow up and become adults, in other words, to become independent. For once that happens it is no longer possible to think of them as permanent dolls or playthings. Throughout the period during which the child is growing up this sort of clinging to the early stage of his development on the part of the mother is going to cramp the evolution of his emotional life. Nevertheless, the evolution is going on in spite of her, and in the nature of things there will be, sooner or later and sometimes very quickly, a reaction on the part of the child that will provoke in his mother the reflex to regain control over him at just the worst possible time. Then, much later on, when the "doll" has become an adult himself, he will possibly experience some considerable difficulty in extricating himself from this "mother hen" so that he may ensure his own free and personal existence as a man.

All that, though it is cited only as an example, needs to be said all the same; it is not unnatural that many mothers should suffer from this mixture of good and generous intentions and unconscious possessive reactions. It is merely regrettable; and it is good, indeed, to recognize these facts so that mothers may strive to prevent their "feelings" from carrying them away, and try to cultivate an unselfish attitude toward their children.

Then, again, this possessive tendency which persists in parents is perhaps the most trying obstacle in the path of a fruitful religious education, but it is a phenomenon found so generally that it has colored current expressions to the extent that people do not realize when such expressions become quite wrong. Where are the parents who have not declared at some time: "My son, or my daughter, is very good; or works very well; he, or she, will make us very proud. . . ." An interpretation could be placed upon these commonplaces of current speech. In other words, it is as if the children were destined to be the witnesses to the high educative qualities of their parents. . . . There is nothing more egoistic, in fact, than such affirmations. Children exist for their own sakes and to take their active places in the Mystical Body of Christ. That they bring honor or otherwise to their parents is of so little importance as to be negligible. This is all the more so when the parents, finite beings themselves, possess a conception of "honor" and what it represents which may perhaps be good but which is severely limited by their own outlook. Again, that outlook itself, outside of whatever teaching they have themselves received, is conditional upon their personal unconscious and on the prejudices of their social class or "family clan." For example: what is a good child? He is the child who does not annoy or irritate grownups who are visiting his home; who remains still and quiet ("children only speak when they are spoken to"), in such a way that people will be able to admire his nice new clothes which he has not soiled by playing, or the "excellent upbringing" he has received. . . . In fact, this "good child" is literally an unnatural horror: a child can only be "good" in this way when he has become a man and is capable of clear thinking and detachment. It is quite another matter to ask of a child, on a visit, for example, not to annoy the grown-ups through love for them. But even then it is a good thing to know when to give some outlet adapted to the child's normal need for action, for play and for daydreaming. . . .

Another example, though very different, demonstrates this same possessiveness. We are thinking of the overanxious mother who surrounds her son or her daughter with pullovers and scarves, with woolly bed socks and a dozen other protections against the elements for fear that they will catch something, chiefly through contact with the children of other families unknown to her and considered because of this as a species of ragamuffins or tramps. She has such a fear of "losing" them. But one "loses" only something that belongs to one.

In other words, the child is not some *thing* which belongs to his parents, as we have already stressed. He is already a person who has his own destiny in God's plan. We are looking at things through Christian eyes, since this is a study of the subject of religious education. From the Christian standpoint when a child dies, he is not "lost"; he takes his place in a mysterious community, animated by God Himself, where his parents also must have their own places. Neither does he become "an angel in heaven," a puerile expression in much use among feeble-minded grownups, but he lives in the true light and has taken his permanent place in readiness for the Resurrection. To be rigorously logical it is unbecoming for the Christian adult to say things like: "I have lost my father, or my wife, or my son. . . ." The proper expression would be simply: "My father is dead. . . ."

This does not mean that the suffering, sometimes extremely acute, brought about by such separations in time is wrong in itself and ought to be repressed. The Christian logic consists precisely in the paradox of accepting suffering lucidly in order to discover its ultimate significance and in rising above the persistent recurrences of this possessive egoism which we all drag along with us in greater or lesser degree.

It would seem that more habitual and more theological contemplation on what takes place in God could help parents upon this matter. For it is in God that generation is found in the pure and absolutely perfect state: the Father begets the Word in the Unity of the Holy Spirit. But He begets at the beginning and from all eternity the Equal of Himself, absolutely distinct and absolutely equal, since the Word is God Himself and yet God is One because He is Absolute Love. There cannot be between these two Persons any difference of time or greatness of worth. There can be only the exchange of a pure and total relationship. The One engenders, the Other is engendered. It is the exact opposite of possession.

Where is the human father who, from the birth of his child, conscientiously concerns himself only with helping his child to be his equal, independent and free before God? Yet this should be the most normal and most elementary requirement of the role of father. It is for parents to understand the necessity for overcoming methodically and progressively the egocentric reflexes of possessiveness that they still retain in the unconscious turmoil of their emotional life.

Projecting Parental Ambitions

Another problem is that of projections. This problem is somewhat different although it does highlight a certain form of possessiveness or, in other words, the reduction of the child to the status of an object.

Here again a single example will be more illumi-

nating than a long theoretical dissertation. Let us take
the case of a man of about forty, the father of a
family, whose personal life has always been tinged
with nostalgia and disappointment. He would have
liked to have been a naval officer, but his own father,
either an uncomprehending type or else not having
the necessary means to fulfill his son's wish, had
turned him in the direction of the family business:
the father was a horse dealer. (Let it be observed in
passing that this worthy individual had never had
the necessary drive or resilience to try to achieve
his aim for himself, even though he could have done
so. This denotes *a priori* a certain emotional defeat
in his own childhood, and further a source of later
reactions more emotional than rational in the direction of his personal frustrations.) He begets a son
in his own turn. And he decrees with sublime
naïveté that his son shall succeed where he failed:
he shall be a naval officer. Only the boy, launched
against all his own personal likes and tastes upon
the study of mathematics which weighs intolerably
upon him, dreams of a very different career: he is
passionately interested in nature, in agriculture and
in breeding, and his one ideal, which is perfectly
legitimate, is to be a horse dealer. . . . A veritable
conspiracy between his various mentors and advisers
and the influential members of his family must be
formed if this fifteen-year-old is to be saved from
such paternal folly.

A case like this, which is completely authentic, is
not at all rare. Moreover, the parents at the other
end of the scale who really know how to discover,
guide and encourage the real tastes of their children,
unexpected or disappointing though they may be,
are in the minority. Now religious education must
be directed to the advancement of the personality
of the child so that he may himself be able to enter
upon personal relationship of faith and of love with

God. Therefore such suppression of natural and perfectly legitimate aspirations cannot but compromise very seriously the religious maturity of the future adult.

Among parents there is the tendency, very general and very strong, to desire more or less unconsciously that their children should make a success of whatever, in their own subjective world, they themselves have dreamed of realizing. But here again this is a strangely egocentric point of view. The children themselves will have to achieve whatever they desire. Education consists essentially in providing them with the elements, both emotional and intellectual, of sane judgment, as independent as possible of the emotional and limited world of their parents.

We were speaking of the projection of the father upon his son, but we could say as much upon the subject of the projection of the mother upon her daughter. For example, the mother is peculiarly sensitive in the matter of her daughter's marriage. The inviolable and secret unity of the young couple, so strongly demanded in Genesis, in the Gospels and in St. Paul, counts for very little in the face of the excessive invasions of the mother-in-law who aspires, though without realizing it, to live vicariously by means of her daughter a conjugal experience that will compensate for her own which has, unfortunately, fallen below the ideal, however unrealistic, that she had pictured for herself.

Sometimes this projection of parents upon their children takes on an aspect of refined and unconscious cruelty which could easily be qualified as sadistic, and it is not so rare as one might think. The various distressing facts that come to light about child martyrs are, in fact, only the spectacular angle of it. In the past life of every human being there will inevitably be found periods which were unhappy, even sorrowful, and all the good will of their families will never prevent this inescapable fact: a *perfectly* happy childhood does not exist nor could it. Consequently there will appear in the adult a spontaneous and very general reaction, even though often it is not formulated: the adult will tend to relive in the children with whom he has to deal the experiences which he himself lived through, to "have his revenge" in some way for whatever wrongs he suffered. This attitude sometimes take on just a slight hint of a pseudo-moral outlook which deceptively persuades the parent that he is motivated purely by justice and equality. "I was thwarted and made angry in my time, and it is just that you should be so, too," speaks the unconscious of the father, who can only recall his own hard childhood in this retributive vein. This is a terrible extreme of self-centeredness that takes as its scale of values and the norm of its supreme and absolute comparison a man's own personal experience.

Where this outlook prevails everything goes on just as if the parents could not bear that their children should be happier than they were themselves, or attain to a level of culture or of development and fulfillment which they never reached. It is the exact opposite of the preceding reaction, but it is also very common. In general, however, it is better camouflaged because it is more sordid and less idealistic. It will be expressed in aphorisms, the psychological exegesis of which still remains to be made, of the following type: "I was brought up like this and I haven't done so badly; there is no point in changing things." Or again: "If people are going to start changing their ideas about education where will it all stop?" The danger here would appear to be all the more serious because it is more subtly dissimulated under the guise of a most solemn and righteous loyalty to what are called traditions, but which are nothing more nor less than prejudices. The infinite need for reflection and adaptation required for a successful approach to real life is dangerously misunderstood; and the virtue of prudence which generates this very power of reflection and of adaptation, a cardinal virtue into the bargain, is directly negated.

We may add to the foregoing all the unconscious bases that can be found: the anguish of mistaken guilt in regard to the superego; [1] the "jealousy" of the father who from the point of view of character is lacking in virility and who persecutes, though without realizing it, the more complete virility of his sons; the mother who finds it impossible to accept the fact that her daughters are blossoming in a feminine way of life which she herself never fully accepted, again without her realizing it.

Certain readers may feel a little scandalized by such statements. Let us, however, reiterate once more that there is no question here of conscious sentiments, fully recognized and deliberately accepted; and therefore no question of *moral* crimes. But it is essential, all the same, to bear clearly in mind that we all carry within us, and none knew this better than the great saints, *unconscious* evils. These correspond in actual psychology to that which in theology we recognize as the damaged condition of man, and against which our moral conscience has continually to struggle. Surely the best thing is courageously to admit the presence of these evils. It would seem, in all reasonableness, that this would be one of the most effective ways of preventing ourselves from being misled by them.

Transference

Under the name of transference a third problem could be mentioned here, inasmuch as it bears some relationship to the problem of possessiveness.

The emotional life of the human being contains

always certain zones of frustration or lack of fulfillment. When such dissatisfaction is consciously apprehended there will be a certain amount of suffering that is borne more or less well, according to one's spiritual outlook upon life. But when such frustration is unconscious, or when it has been quickened into life within the unconscious mind, the person concerned will seek instinctively and without understanding, at least at the outset, to find some object that will fill the void and thanks to which he will be able to escape from this sensation of nostalgia. In other words when a person comes along who corresponds in certain ways to whatever the person concerned unconsciously lacks, the subject will revive a want, an emotional thirst, of which he may be only tardily aware, and still in a superficial way, without being able to relate these feelings to their true source.

This psychological process, extremely common though in varying degrees, can appear very strongly in the relationship of parents toward their children. However, in most cases it never goes beyond the level of a slight and passing uneasiness, or of certain manifestations of affection which are slightly disproportionate or unsuitable in quality. Nevertheless, the problem does sometimes go deeper and carry more serious consequences with it.

Here again the best method of explanation is an example chosen for its explicitness and for the fact that it corresponds to one of the commonest forms of this psychological process. Let us imagine a woman who, in the course of her own emotional development, has accumulated certain little conflicts in regard to the acceptance of her femininity by the men with whom she has come in contact since her early childhood; her father to begin with, then one or other of her brothers, then this or that young man from her own group of friends in adolescence or young womanhood. It becomes a matter, then, of sexual conflict, unconscious and repetitive, not precisely in the genital or erotic sense of this word, but in the larger sense of the general psychology of the fact of sexuality itself and all that it means. This girl then marries. It is very probable that these previous conflicts will remain unsolved in the course of her conjugal life which will not itself be able to fill the emotional voids that persist in her unconscious. She has a son. Now the relations are reversed. For the first time this woman finds herself in the presence of a male who touches her closely, who represents virtual, complete virility right from his birth, and who is a child while she is an adult. The opportunity is here offered for such a woman's unconscious emotions to seek in this "man" who has been born of her, who is part of her, all that she failed to find in other men, not excepting her husband. The expression "unconscious incest" comes to mind, even though it is in fact wholly inadequate for the simple reason that it implies a qualifying moral responsibility, while this situation, as we said earlier, is one of *unconscious* reaction reflexes.

This is a situation that can be expressed by a thousand different actions on the part of the mother, all tending to make use of her son as an object of compensation. What is more, it is a situation which does not conduce toward a deepening of the conjugal communion between her husband and herself. The most obvious consequence of it will be a certain tendency to keep her son in a prolonged state of childhood. That is to say, she will want him to be a man, but one from whom there is nothing to fear so long as she can go on "cherishing" him, and to keep him the kind of dependent man who will not try to "break loose" or look elsewhere for interests thereby frustrating his mother all over again in a matter that is both confused and yet intense, and in which frustration is well-nigh intolerable. Here again, from the point of view of religious education, the risks are serious: such prolonged infantilism in her son's development is not likely to assist the growth of his liberty and his autonomy; and these are the only psychological foundations upon which he can progressively construct an authentic attitude in his unique relationship with God.

The mothers who read this work should not seize upon this matter to upset themselves or to cause themselves serious anxiety or scruples. Such unconscious mechanisms are extremely common but they reach the pathological intensity of the "genitrix" in only the rarest of cases. It is sufficient to know that these transferences are always possible in some slight form; here again it is of primary importance for us to learn how to overcome them without being shaken and how to become imbued a little more, at each stage in the lives of our sons, with the words of Genesis: "A man shall leave father and mother, and shall cleave to his wife; and they shall be two in one flesh." It sometimes seems as though it is the very mothers who are deeply involved in this sort of situation who are tempted to give vent to indignation and protest violently: "This is not possible. . . ." It is always very painful to face something that will cause personal suffering without understanding; to accept it calmly would be to resolve it.

There are many forms of transference which could appear in the relationships of parents and children: the mother and her son, the mother and her daughter; the father and his daughter, the father and his son. They can also arise in the relationship which prevails between the teacher and the student. . . .

The primary condition for a positive educational attitude on this point is obviously a lucid knowledge

of it, as of all the possible manifestations of the unconscious. These things are the commonplaces of
human life. And any educational approach that takes
theoretical cognizance of the dogma of original sin
and yet neglects to bear in mind the real and practical
repercussions of this mystery in the psychological
make-up of the educators themselves, wuld be gravely
compromised by something very closely resembling
pride.

IV
Emotional Evolution
—Its Requirements

W<small>E</small> now come to a stage in these reflections at which we might conveniently make a quick survey of the findings of modern science on the subject of the psychological evolution of the child. These findings are, for the most part, reasonably new although they are assuming an ever-growing importance in a number of studies in the fields of medicine, social service, rehabilitation and so on.

There can be no question here of doing more than recalling them in very general terms so that the conceptions which people customarily possess about the psychology of the child and its evolution may be brought more into conformity with what actually takes place.

Two aspects strike us at the outset: first, the essentially dynamic and progressive development of what we call the formation of the personality; second, the primordial importance of the emotional life and of its elaboration along this progressive line. But it is essential that there should be an understanding of what comprises the *emotional life* in the child at all the early stages. In fact, when talking of this life we are forced to use terms which correspond rather to the sentiments of adults, and such terms are obviously inadequate. In fact, in the emotional life of the child it is not so much a matter of sentiments but rather of reactions, of an emotional kind indefinable in themselves and not capable of being formulated in exact terms, for the very simple reason that they cannot yet be clearly conscious and therefore capable of being analyzed. It is enough that each one of us should cast his or her mind back to our own childhood in order to understand this point. These emotional reactions do present a certain analogy with adult feelings of which they are really no more than a kind of "confused prefiguration," and that is why we have to give them the same label; but that remains, in a certain sense, a necessary convention. To say, for example, that a child of two years experiences reactions of jealousy toward his little brother who was born recently must be altered to saying that "his behavior would indicate that he was jealous," that there is in his make-up *something which resembles* jealousy.

If the first characteristic of this emotional life then is that it is not clearly conscious or accessible for the time being to reason, the second aspect, which is a consequence of the first, will be the characteristics of intensity and of transience. Any fear, for example, in the case of the little child is a total drama in which his reason, still in the limbo of the potential, cannot help him to appreciate either the exact proportions or the transient nature of the thing that frightens him. The child, because of his sensibility which is wholly alive and eager, cannot yet have a sense of relative values any more than he can have a knowledge of the change in the seasons; for such knowledge requires a reflexive experience impossible before the child has reached a certain age. Thus the child is wholly absorbed in the intensity of the moment, the here and now, without any possible nuances. Rational control of the emotional world is, in fact, a far more progressive and later development than most adults imagine.

In this fact, too, is to be found one of the difficulties of the work of education: the difficulty of trying to understand what really is the psychological life of the child of three, four or five years. The adult has actually forgotten what this is for the very reason that he was not himself clearly conscious of his own first emotional experiences. The effort to "re-understand" the infantile world is of fundamental usefulness from many points of view. First of all, metaphysical reflection, properly so called, upon man in general, cannot be artificially rationalized into a theoretical ideal. But above all, in what concerns our thesis, its importance is of the first account to education which is principally religious. For instance, if a child experiences in a brutal or in a repeated way an emotion that paralyzes his emotional dynamism at its actual level of evolution, the very intensity of this emotion instead of guiding him will cause the emotion to persist in the unconscious, so that one variable part of the dynamism of his personality will remain "twisted," retarded, and not disposed to receive the supreme and supernatural gift of the Faith.

General Trends of Emotional Evolution

Before recalling in quick review the different stages of the emotional evolution of the child, we should prefer to outline its general trends. One could say, though of necessity in a somewhat arbitrary and theoretical way, that the first seven or eight years of childhood witness a kind of rapid and intense fermentation of emotional experiences that strongly conditions the bases of the child's future life. Later comes adolescence, which takes up, in a somewhat crucial stage of development, the elements thus supplied.

At the outset of his existence the child is a sort of indistinct, reactive entity; his sensibility is not individualized initially by any connection with those who surround him; his own interior universe is not divided into distinct component parts and the harmonious relations of these components are not realized. The emotional evolution will consist at the outset—and this is perhaps its most important aspect—in a series of distinct, successive *zones*, first sensory and corporal, then psychic and emotional, in the emotional consciousness of the subject, who proceeds to "invest" therein progressively something of himself. Thus progressively, and at a rate slightly behind that of the biological development the spirit will be able to assume at its own transcendent level, mysterious but undeniable, these "investments" into a reflexive knowledge that is totally different from a purely sensory knowledge. It will be able to direct them (unequally, of course, in accordance with the failures always possible in this evolution) in the action of the free will which is in the strongest sense of the word *personal*.

It is quite evident that the more successfully the first stages of "investment" have been normally passed, the more the unconscious emotional content and reflexes of the subject will be amenable to the spirit.

Findings of Clinical Psychology

There are two types of readers who run the risk of experiencing either anxiety or irritation when they come to the following pages. First of all, there are those who are well informed about the horizons opened up by contemporary psychology. What follows will probably appear to them slight and theoretical, if not actually oversimplified. But they are better placed than others for understanding that one cannot deal adequately with such problems in the space of one short chapter. The theme or argument of this book does not consist in this but rather in reflections on certain particular aspects of religious education. Nevertheless, it was necessary that we make, for those who know very little about them, some mention of such psychological data.

But of course these readers, too, risk a certain form of reaction to these pages. This account could seem to them, at the worst, fantastic, something like the wild imaginings of psychologists badly in need of some novel approach. These actual findings of clinical psychology require to be progressively approached, carefully graded and abundantly illustrated by concrete examples if they are to be properly understood. The necessarily brief and somewhat abrupt nature of this chapter may therefore be a cause of offense to some.

It has seemed essential to us to include it, however, no matter how great the danger of this is. So we would ask of our readers that they make the effort to approach it with good will and a certain amount of indulgence. The first type of reader could merely glance through it for it will not bring them anything of great importance. . . . The second type would do well to remind themselves that the chapter is little more than an outline, quite slight and insufficient for real study, designed solely to draw their attention to the whole subject, and to indicate the fact that here is a whole field of human knowledge only newly discovered and explored, and to give them, also, a desire to learn more about it.

Furthermore, it is necessary to insist upon the inadequate and debatable nature of the vocabulary available to us for a discussion of this subject. This vocabulary is derived directly from the Freudian school and that in itself is enough to shock some. The psychology known as Freudian was, of course, initiated by the works of Freud *as a doctor*—in other words it is a system in the medical and clinical sense of this word, and not in the mathematical sense of an exact science. It has, in fact, already passed far beyond the limits of Freud's own works, though remaining faithful to the spirit of the genius who opened up the way to this type of knowledge. One could hardly, I think, better compare this pioneer work than by likening it to the scientific vistas—on a very different plane—opened up by the brilliant discoveries of Pasteur.

It is not a question here of philosophy but of the science of observation. There are some people who, for vastly differing reasons, cannot tolerate the fact that one should make any allusion, whatever it may be, to Freudian psychology. Allow us to express the opinion that this reaction is somewhat excessive. Certainly, on the medical plane, one cannot agree with his psychoanalytical explanations of neuroses. But that is not the matter for discussion here. The fact is that the psycho-affective evolution of the child is made according to certain rhythms and certain stages of importance that are by no means negligible. One is obliged, even if referring to them only briefly, to accept the working hypothesis established by the ideas and the terminology of Freudian psychology. But of course it must be realized that this is only a necessary convention, a "manner of speaking" because we need one to express realities in themselves inexpressible, and because this is still the only truly adequate technical language at our disposal.

Food

The first stage then is confused, chaotic, comparable to the shapelessness of a nebula. It is entirely centered around the primordial need of the child at this period: food. All emotional satisfaction, whether agreeable or painful, is in one piece, so to speak, involving the relaxation or the contraction of all the sensory registers at the same time, according to the satisfaction or non-satisfaction of this need. For discrimination to begin normally later on, it is logically necessary that the infant should live through this period with the satisfying of his wants predominating over the non-satisfying of them. Unless this is the case, one part of the evolutionary process would have to remain undeveloped or retarded. In a sense, then, we should even go so far as to say that the primary chronological condition of a successful future evolution is actually implicit in the nursing role of the mother. All the psychologists agree in emphasizing the importance of maternal affection in these early days of life, or at least upon the suitable replacement of that affection if it is not available.

It is the whole problem of children put out to nurse that their original situation is always jeopardized, to a very grave extent with later conflict if there is any period of abandonment, with less grave risks if the mother's place is suitably filled. Equally so they are in agreement that the ideal age for transition to weaning is about the age of six months. We should not forget that at this stage the emotions are profoundly "visceral" and easily take on an indelible character in the unconscious of the adult. A child who has seriously lacked the affection of a nursing mother in the early months of his existence suffers grave risks to his corporal and psychic health. And since the fullest expansion and development of the religious sentiment are the supernatural climax of man's normal evolution, it is eminently desirable that his equilibrium should not be exposed to danger at the start, and that his religious sentiment should not be diverted from its living sources to the point of leaving him impervious to the transcendent action of God which is essential to his right attitude toward the Faith.

Inadequate satisfaction of the primitive emotional need of the child is as damaging as a too prolonged extension of this need by overlate weaning. Psychopathology demonstrates this abundantly every day.

This is not by any means a psychologist's dream or the workings of his imagination. The child at the dawn of his existence has an *oral* need of his mother which requires sufficient but not too much satisfaction, so that his later development can begin under the best conditions. And remote though it may appear, one of the starting points of a religious education is to be found in maternal nursing under the most balanced emotional conditions possible. The human being is a dynamic unity, complex but indivisible, and it is necessary to know how to look to a child's future development. This is indeed for parents a primary demand of love.

First Emotional Experiences

Next in the imperceptible and yet rapid procession of transitionary stages there follows the stage where the child encounters the first emotional experiences of his own potential actions.

Influenced by training in cleanliness, combined with the spontaneous evolution of his own psyche, the child discovers, in his confused organic sensitiveness, a new satisfaction from the mastery of his sphincters and the corporal sensations which it entails. In analogical terms (see above) one could say that the child, for the first time so far in his existence, discovers little by little an obscure satisfaction, both physical and emotional, from causing, of his own free will, the evacuation of something from himself, something the form of which depends on him. This discovery is accomplished by reflexes easily discernible to the experienced eye: the first outline of an attitude of offering (generally to his mother) together with a certain anguished sense of loss of his own substance. This stage marks the taking root, although in a very obscure and confused state, of the instinct of aggressiveness; namely of a dynamism that later on, having been fitted into its proper place in the light of the spirit, will be the actual force of creativeness in all domains, and of exchanges with the rest of the human race.

The easy and successful transition through this stage is important for the development of the child's personal attitude in later life: it is the emotional point of departure for a flexible and dynamic activity. If the distress of the sense of loss predominates there will be engrafted in the unconscious a panic fear of painful sanctions, or if the first slight attempt at self-offering is misunderstood or rejected by those around him, it is always possible that the result will be an emotional unbalance in the action of the child that will hinder his human and religious expansion even if this should take only the form of "nervous" refusal to accept setbacks, the prerequisite of progress, or death which is the prerequisite of resurrection.

There next follows the stage when the awareness of the child invests his sexual individuality with the quality of distinctiveness. That is to say, he discovers to some degree a territory of his emotional-sensory life that is linked to the mystery of what is perhaps the strangest of all his adult potentialities—an existential power of procreative love. It is of the highest importance that this stage should not be marked by any sort of superstitious or ritualistic fear, so that the adolescent, later the adult, will be able to integrate the power of his sexual instinct in a full and rounded vision of his own proper place, purpose and importance. In other words he may later, if he so desires, make the decision to develop in himself the virtue of true chastity, which means the relating of his vital powers to Love properly so called, which is God.

It is also of the highest importance that the child should perceive the difference between the sexes. Moreover, he should accept his own sexual condition

as a boy—or a girl should be adjusted to her stand-
ing as a female—without the slightest suggestion of
either superiority or inferiority but purely as a characteristic, individual and personal, fully valuable and
relative or more exactly *relational,* or in other words,
in perfect harmony of relationship with the rest of
mankind. The important aspect of this stage is that
the anatomic genital reality, to which the child of
three or four years old spontaneously attaches an
intense emotional interest, should be only *symbolic,*
in fact, of the condition of man or of woman, and
the component characteristics which that entails. A
child who has a fear of his own sex, in the emotional
and symbolical sense of this term, will always be
more or less hindered later on, first in being satisfied
with what he is and then in his task of developing a
positive religious and Christian attitude in the mastery of his sensual nature. In order to emphasize
this we could cite striking instances of those dramas
of conscience which among young people, as among
men and women of mature years, are in fact rooted
in an emotional unbalance dating from this stage of
their phychological growth.

The "Oedipus" Conflict

The modern psychology of dynamisms next deals
with another stage for which no one has yet found
any other designation than an allusion to an ancient
Hellenic myth; that is the "oedipus" conflict. At
this stage, which according to the psychologists is
about the age of four, five or six years, the sensory
reactions, whose starting point is corporal, are no
longer the ones influencing the child. For the first
time the question is one of pure psychological affec-
tivity, though the subject is not clearly conscious of
this at all. Physical or sensory circumstances are no

longer directly concerned. The affective psychic "zone" invested at this stage is twofold: first of all the child is beginning in a confused way to feel his status as a social subject; and second, this is in accordance with the sex to which he belongs and whose specific character he is beginning positively to accept. For the first time—and, let us repeat, in an emotional and non-rational manner—he experiences social reality as a boy or as a girl, as the case may be. The peak of his early childhood, this period is of basic importance. One could say that the majority of later difficulties in social and conjugal adjustment are rooted more or less there.

Up to this the child was passively dependent upon the milieu in which he lived, that is, upon his parents. The boy always has been directly and above all dependent upon his mother; the girl, once she has been freed from the early maternal proximity connected with her nourishment, equally directly and above all upon her father. In this there is a natural relationship of a complementary kind, confused but nevertheless very deep-seated. In a review of the situation one might then say that the child at this stage is normally fixed passively and in a predominant way on the parent of the other sex. But this fixation and this need have already been actually experienced in the way of which we spoke at the beginning of this chapter: emotional, absolute and without possible inward sharing. Then comes the moment when the child is faced with the necessity of accepting this sharing: in other words, he now discovers the importance of the parent of the same sex as himself in relation to the other parent. His father and his mother, he sees, form, apart from his existence, a stable and united world of which he is not the center but the outcome. His first reflex will be to refuse what he resents as a dramatic threat to his deepest security. He will then "react against" the parent of the same sex as himself, to try to "dissociate" the parental group by reactions all the more violent in that they are repressed, since he feels them as vaguely threatening in themselves. In adult terms we should say: "It is dangerous to tackle a rival of such proportions. . . ."

In normal family conditions these reactions will come up against an impossibility, which will force the child to emerge from his drama by a forward step in his evolution. He then *"accepts"* the social fact (the communion of two people who love each other) and he will find the means of taking his own place in this relationship and thereby preparing himself, in a kind of instinctive manner, for his own future role: he begins to identify himself with the parent of the same sex as himself, with what will permit him to succeed in his own turn in achieving a comparable destiny. To put it in yet another way, this stage is for the child the first real renunciation of his previous primitive way, the purely egocentric way, of sensation and feeling, and therefore his first positive preparation for a later possibility of true love. The aspect of the "assent to the social relationship" along the lines of his own sexual status is by far the most important in our study: the Christian life is precisely love supernaturally enlarged in charity, in the framework of the community *par excellence* which is the Mystical Body of Christ.

All that has just been said is obviously merely the meaning or significance, insofar as our adult reason can formulate it, of what takes place, in fact, in the emotional life of the child and which is, once again, inexpressible in adequate terms. But it would be very serious to fail to recognize, because of this, a complex psychological reality through which of necessity every child must pass, whether or not it can be expressed in clear signs. What is more, many of the "childish sayings" that people are apt to find purely quaint or amusing could assume, in this light, a very eloquent meaning.

Adolescence

The last stage of the child's evolution, when his emotions ripen to maturity, takes place at the time of the start of adolescence. But at this period the consciousness is awake, so are reason and the spiritual power of reflection which have been expanding during the period known as latency (roughly speaking, between the ages of eight and twelve years): school age, relatively and provisionally speaking, is the period during which the stabilization of the emotional evolution takes place; the faculties of the mind and spirit then come into play and the period is a decisive one.

The instinctive energies, under the biological urge of puberty, burst forth in their last stage of development with the dramatic force of a storm shattering a serene sky. The sexual instinct, like the instinct of aggression, reaches practically the level of its full adult potentiality. This time the manifestations reach through to the conscious mind. Obviously, of course, this transition carries nothing essentially new with it: the instinctual energies have been, during all the childhood stages of development, already oriented and somewhat confusedly conditioned by their reactions. It is only to a certain extent a kind of resumption, though of course of a far more intense quality, and with the full grasp by the conscious mind, of the manifestations of the earlier stages of development and evolution. The adolescent is reaching the threshold of his true autonomy: he—or she—is on the point of becoming a man or a woman who is capable of participating in his or her own chosen line of action, no longer in the old scholastic or family milieu, but in the world of others. This is already to say at what point the educative task is important, above all as regards the long-term preparation of the elements of this crisis of adolescence. It is to say too, in passing, how indispensable it is to furnish the child, above all from the sexual point of view, with the elements of information that are essential for him to understand and to direct according to his will all that is happening within himself.

This is the more necessary in that the subject, who is no longer a child, properly speaking, and who is not yet completely an adult, experiences a very genuine disturbance, sometimes quiescent and sometimes acute, during the two or three years of the first phase of adolescence. He is uneasy deep down in himself, so to speak. On the one hand he feels a very deep-seated attraction toward this new world he is discovering and in which he is tending toward taking his own place; on the other there is a profound emotional reaction which one could only compare with terror, in the face of the intimidating unknown that this represents. There is also a kind of nostalgia, sometimes explicit and acute, for the old condition of childhood whose advantages and relative tranquillity he knows very well by experience.

The ebb and flow of this very deep and intense conflict that marks the process of maturing are normally expressed by ill-adapted reactions, by a retreat into himself and by an instinctive opposition to the family milieu. Frequently some traces of the old "oedipus" conflict will awaken, and the opposition may take the form of a hostile relationship with the parent of the same sex. At one time the enthusiasm for going forward into the "unknown" will predominate and there will be excessive reactions, more passionate than reflective, of independence or of the desire for creation. At other times it will be the distress or the nostalgia that will take over, and will

in its turn produce regressions or exaggerated egocentric demands.

This is the "ungrateful" age, uncomfortable for the
subject's family and companions undoubtedly, but
considerably more uncomfortable for the adolescent
going through it. It will be very necessary for parents, doing their best to recall the days of their own
adolescence, to realize that there is very little they
can do. Often it is a good time to "hand on the job"
to someone outside the immediate family circle:
teacher, friend, head of a youth movement, or a
priest. . . . They should realize, also, and this is a
difficult task, that they should respect the coming to
fruition of the freedom of this new adult, since they
can no longer do as much as they were able to do in
childhood to guide and correct it. Above all else it is
essential for them to accept the fact that their child
is beginning quite legitimately to "escape" from them,
or, in other words, is becoming that ever intriguing
mystery, an autonomous individual. It is at the
period of the adolescence of their children that all the
little problems of the parents' unconscious are revived: they feel, in fact, that they are being fatally
frustrated in their "object."

A true case history here will also be an effective
illustration. In a particular family of very strong
practicing Christians and of a high level of culture
and education the eldest of the five children, a youth
of between seventeen and eighteen years of age, announced one day that he had lost the Faith, that he
would never again set foot inside a church nor take
part in any religious services or practices, for to him,
henceforth they would mean nothing more than hypo-
critical shams. In the face of an obviously calm and
clear set of mind, his parents by mutual consent decided that it would be a better thing to say nothing
and to respect this crisis. Never once on a Sunday,
despite the strongest desire to do so, did his mother

venture to say: "Will you come to Mass with us?"
Throughout the course of many years, while continuing to live their own daily Christian life as sincerely
as possible, the parents had the united and very un-
common courage never to bear down in any way on
the conscience of the young man. Outwardly nothing
was happening: then, when he was about twenty-six
years of age and had just completed a brilliant course
of university study, he announced that after mature
reflection he had made up his mind to enter a Bene-
dictine monastery. To his astonished parents he
added the comment: "I can tell you now that if you
had not shown the respect for my liberty of judgment
that you did I don't know if I should have ever found
the Faith again." An example like this is striking in
the extreme. But it is deplorable that this type of
parental reaction to the conflicts of adolescence is so
rare; it denotes a singular educative aptitude in that
father and mother, for it rounds off very logically all
their previous attitudes to their children.

Receptivity to Divine Revelation

The real problem, of course, in regard to religious
education, is to know in what way the child is most
receptive to the Divine Revelation, not indeed according to the theories of the textbooks which correspond
to the mentalities of intellectual adults, but in direct
relation to the particular psychological development
of each individual.

It is a delicate enough problem. For if it is desirable that this Revelation should be satisfying or
suitable to the particular stage of receptivity of the
child, it is at least as important that education should
not set bounds to this Revelation at a transitory
stage; it matters, above all, that the presentation
made of it should not remain at a childish level, nei-

ther in vocabulary nor in spirit nor in intellectual content. There is grave risk under such conditions of preparing the way for a later, possibly serious, crisis in adolescence or young adulthood in which the subject indignantly rejects notions he considers puerile (quite rightly since they have been allowed to remain so) and customs that seem ridiculous to him.

We shall return in a later chapter to the very real importance of the "father" element for the discovery of God. But the "mother" element also plays a considerable role. When a little boy of about five years of age is told about the Blessed Virgin, for example, and there is not much said about St. Joseph, the story that he is told is quite likely to coincide with the "oedipus" stage and to be taken up in connection with that. The essentially mysterious quality of the motherhood of Our Lady is in danger of being absorbed in a sort of compensatory way in the unformulated conflict that is being waged, and as an emotional conception in cases where this conflict has been resolved along the lines of the aggressive instinct which rebels against the parental couple. If care is not taken here such emotional coloring will become a part of the general conception and will hinder the child who attains school age from understanding, if indeed anyone seeks to explain to him, that such a conception has nothing to do with Our Lady: that the motherhood of Mary is a supernatural reality without any comparison with human motherhood, which is on the plane of the senses and the emotions. When he reaches twenty years of age, and has come into contact with the toughness and the ignorance of the world, he will then have nothing substantial in his mind to forestall an ironical attitude toward something which is only a caricature without consistency.

If, at the other extreme, religion is presented to him as nothing more than a series of prohibitions intended to make him "good"—we have already translated this as meaning "not to be a nuisance to the grownups" — his susceptibilities will all have been handled in a way contrary to his quite legitimate desires and the *religious* dimension, not the "moral" one, of his life will have nothing favorable or attractive about it, so that it will be perfectly natural for him in later years to throw off such a stultifying and totally inadequate "net" of abstract constraints. Too many young people, accustomed in their childhood to *obligatory* attendance at Mass on days other than Sundays declare on entering on a university career that they "have had enough of Mass to last them a lifetime. . . ." It is very stupid reasoning, of course; we know that; but what weapons have they been provided with to fight it?

They are lucky, too, if no one mixes up with the "first rudiments" of their religion the nonsensical legend of Santa Claus. In making the thing simple for themselves and satisfying their own eternal childishness, the parents construct a characteristic lie around the pure and absolute receptivity of the little child. Instead of telling him about "Santa Claus" as a little story "not true, of course," they make him *believe* in the coming of this man, a legendary figure who has come straight out of the pagan stories of the Norsemen. One day the child will have to learn that it was only "a joke." But we happen to know of a little boy of six years of age who continued logically: "I see. Then, the Infant Jesus is He 'a joke,' too?" Try to tell him then that Santa Claus and the coming of the Infant Jesus are two different things and that he must be able to discriminate. . . . His confidence has been sapped: people have played with something which was sacred: the fragility of an awakening conscience. Then there is the little child who replies to his skeptical comrades: "But it is true. Daddy said so." He is facing the risk of feeling a most intense anguish that he will not know either how to resolve or to express when he finally realizes that "Daddy" deliberately has fooled him. The repercussions of a stupidity of this kind run the danger of being incalculable and of hanging fire. Regarding the adults who simperingly protest: "Ah, nonsense! It is not so serious as that; it is all just a pretty and amusing little story," they would need to examine their own unconscious a little more closely, as we have already suggested in Chapter III. One cannot play pretty games with a human personality in the process of maturing.

Besides, the adolescent will have to discover God in His transcendence and in His historic and sacramental character. It is indispensable, therefore, that he should realize as early as possible that his parents are not gods. It is a matter in which his parents should do all they can to help, of a progressive opening up toward Someone in relationship with whom the parents are strictly on the same level of true value as their own children or as any other representative of the human race. . . .

An Atmosphere of Security

There is another practical consequence of modern dynamic psychology that is rich in material for reflection. The normal elaboration and development of the psyche of children, and therefore their proper balance from both a human and a religious point of view, are essentially conditional upon the solidity, the stability and the calmness of the family environment. In other words, before all else, it is dependent upon the unity and the love of the two parents.

It will be enough to run rapidly over the description of the stages of the emotional life which has just been outlined.

The primary condition for the child to evolve normally in respect of the instinctual conditionings of his psyche is that he should live in an atmosphere of *security*. He is still totally dependent in that he has a fundamental need to feel that his existence is protected and his elementary satisfactions assured; in a word, he needs to be loved. For it is not merely a matter of giving him the right amount of milk or food suited to his age and of ensuring that his essential hygienic requirements are looked after. It is indeed a question of affection, or, in other words, of the "feeling" of the emotional attitude of his parents, that lends to ordinary material care its inimitably human value.

Obviously the first element of such security is the internal security that makes this possible: the unity, that is, of those immediately surrounding the child, in other words, of his parents. In his first months he needs his mother above all else; but it is very clear that she cannot give him the attentive and serene affection he needs unless she herself is quite happy in her conjugal life and her only worries are those of practical day-to-day living. It is all a question of heart: a woman may be deeply burdened with material needs and wants, but if she truly loves and is truly beloved herself, she can, in spite of everything, give her baby all that he, too, needs in the way of love.

In later years the security of the child will have been assured by this serene atmosphere in his childhood home. If he has experienced around him only the ordinary ups and downs that belong to all practical living he will never have the fundamental fear of being abandoned or even threatened in his very existence. It is a striking fact, too, that children are much less disturbed by quick outbursts of temper by parents who genuinely understand and love one another than by the essential dissension in a household that keeps up appearances even in the house and yet is deeply disunited in its very essence or heart. Naturally, systematic agreement is absolutely necessary between father and mother regarding this or that educational course of behavior, or such-and-such an educational sanction, no matter how apparently slight or unimportant. But even more important for the sake of the sensitive and still instinctive awareness of the child is the indefinable atmosphere of balanced affection created by a united home.

It is at the so-called "oedipus" stage that this requirement most obviously shows the sound sense underlying it. The child, indeed, cannot enter positively into this inevitable crisis unless the parent of the same sex seems to him to have a primordial importance in the affections of the parent of the other sex upon whom for the time being, in egocentric fashion, he has a fixation. If this does not happen, he will not *perceive* the social fact of the communion of two people and he will remain, therefore, on the plane of his own instinctual and unconscious emotions, at the reactive stage of the small child. Many of the anti-social or the sometimes extraordinary asocial reactions among certain delinquents, for example, are deeply rooted, as far as unconscious conditionings are concerned, in an "oedipus" stage that was neither entered upon nor liquidated satisfactorily. Careful and enlightened investigation into their past, and especially their childhood years, gives striking evidence of this.

Now this stage of adaptation to the social reality is a fundamental necessity for later adaptation, at the level of the spirit and of the Faith, to the true Christian religious life properly called one of Charity or Love. Religious education does not consist, indeed, solely in getting children to learn their catechism but of encouraging in them, as far as is humanly possible, those potentialities that will become the theological virtues under the action of God. One can only be *totally* Christian if the reality of love and of the communal essence of human nature are not *uncon-sciously* resented as hateful or repulsive.

Religious education will fall on stony ground if the emotional environment in which the child grows up is not normal or not sufficiently balanced. Certainly God will even things up, in the final analysis, if we may use such an expression. But it is contrary to the most elementary logic not to be on one's guard against the accumulation in the child's psyche of obstacles to grace.

When we speak of the stability and the unity of the parents, it is, of course, love to give it its proper name, that we mean. That is to say this dynamic *will* to communion of the one with the other, that has its origin in the spontaneous love emotion, but which goes much further, because consciously, methodically and freely it directs the whole being toward this desirable communion. This obviously demands a continuous effort of self-sacrifice and renunciation on the part of husband and wife in respect of their spontaneous egocentric reactions and sometimes even of their admitted egoisms. . . . This is, moreover, the first condition of their expansion in mutual unity.

It is the couple, *as such,* in mutual unity, who create and educate. It is the love of the couple that is the power of life. There is much to study in the matter of conjugal spirituality, and on this subject the findings of modern psychology could also give considerable help. . . .

To synthesize these different findings one might say that the emotional evolution of the human being consists in a progressive passage, through successive stages, from an *instinctual,* primitive attitude, primarily of the narcissistic type where everything is turned in upon the subject, to an *instinctual* giving and serving attitude harmoniously adjusted to others. This is the normal process and one that is eminently desirable; it could be well described as the "socialization of tendencies."

It is very clear that if one does not wish to end up in an untenable contradiction between the personal, developing life in the future adult and the intellectual ideas that are giving him of a religion entirely centered around Love, it is going to be necessary to take psychological reality into account and to encourage to the utmost this evolution in a normal way. The essential point is never to forget that religious education is not by any means a question of "teaching" solely, but also of a proper psychological atmosphere.

V
The "Superego" and Morality

PEOPLE readily have a tendency to think that the little child, who does not reason, has reactions that are of only slight importance, and that almost suddenly, with the arrival of what is customarily known as "the age of discretion," the sense of good and bad, and then as a consequence, the sense of guilt, are acquired. People have, above all, a tendency to think that the primitive reactions and this sense of guilt are completely unconnected with one another. Actually nothing could be further from the truth. And it is most important to know and to understand this. Otherwise those responsible for educating the child will instill into him a *false* sense of right and wrong and of guilt, that will succeed only in disguising on the conscious plane very primitive reactions of anxiety that are not resolved and are even sustained under the pretext of a supposedly moral education. We say, very rightly, a *false* sense of guilt, by which we mean a psychological attitude that cannot be confused without grave error with the sense of sin and the spiritual and religious attitude of penitence. This latter, of course, is not of the emotional order in its very essence, even though it can derive its origin or have repercussions in the register of the emotions.

To grasp this distinction properly, which is of capital importance in the genesis of a true religious sentiment and therefore in religious education, the best thing to do is to run quickly through what passes in the child's psyche from this point of view. Here again an enlightened observation and study of the unconscious of the adult bring very valuable indications.

The following reflections on the psychogenesis of the instinctive foundations of the future moral conscience cannot perforce be anything but a bare outline. They will merely indicate the existence of a psychological process that is undeniable but very complex. Again, in dealing with this subject we are obliged to use, through lack of other terminology, a technical vocabulary that is as yet poorly developed and that should be looked upon merely as an attempt at expression.

Psychogenisis of Future Moral Conscience

At the start of his life the child, psychologically speaking, is made up of primal dynamisms that correspond to his needs. They are difficult to describe at this period, because they are all mingled in a somewhat confused way and belong to the category of the instincts: they are spontaneous and irrational, and their strong tendency toward immediate satisfaction cannot yet be controlled. The dynamism of the spirit is as yet only "in embryo" and can expand, assuming everything else to be normal, only in proportion to the knowledge the child will acquire of himself and of the world around him.

Yet this knowledge is essentially of a twofold and conflicting quality: one must use the aphorism and say that it is only at peace when it is at war. It is the clash with something other than myself which warns me, sometimes painfully, that I have reached my limits, or to put it in another way, that my territory is precisely and definitely bounded. In that way only can a true relationship between myself and the rest of the world be established; in that way only can I acquire an adequate knowledge of myself and my potentialities. All existence is made up, if we think of it, of this sort of dialectic: when in darkness or obscurity we come up against a wall which serves thereafter to guide us on our way, that is a precise analogy of what is happening.

In all the early days of life this "confrontation" takes place in a purely instinctual and emotional way. And it provokes the formation in the psyche of the child of an instinctive mechanism of opposition to the primitive instincts. Modern psychological terminology designates this psychological reality by the name of "superego." One may argue about the term but the process exists all the same.

The primitive instinct urges the child blindly, and to a certain extent in a less adjusted way than that of animals, toward the satisfaction of a particular need. He clashes with something that forbids this satisfaction and which therefore causes him suffering to a greater or a lesser degree. The need for satisfaction and the fear of the "unpleasant" now start to combine in a kind of interior struggle from which the child will draw, always in the instinctual way, a kind of line of compromise. It is a matter now, in fact, of a proper regulation or canalization of the primitive instinct. But this regulation is made still in the form of instinct and of emotion: fear. In other words, the child assimilates this exterior prohibition into his own interior world of instincts; this becomes, in the guise of an anxiety which is more or less surmountable, a kind of reflex, a prohibition that springs from himself for the same reason, one could say, as the primitive instinct.

This reactive interior system of contra-pulsion, a

somewhat chaotic prefiguration of what later on will be the conscious and rational direction of action, is built up according to the materials at hand. The opacity or the inertia of the material universe, to start with: the glowing stove attracts a child by its bright color, but if he touches it he will be painfully burned; such a very simplified example may help to make this more comprehensible. The world of humans, above all, will present him with numerous and diverse prohibitions and limitations. We would emphasize in passing that these prohibitions and limitations will only too often fluctuate according to the whims of this world of human beings. . . . Just as they will often be dependent variables of the unconscious of individual adults who make up this world, and of prejudices, occasionally revolting it must be stated, of the particular "social environment" or of the "clan." (We are thinking here, for instance, of certain prejudices of class or of race, as much in the sense of "racism" as in the sense of "religious creed.") It must be remembered that the emotions at this age are absolute and intense, without any possible shades or nuances. Thus we may measure the complexity and the importance of the "superego."

It is unnecessary to underline further to what degree this pseudo-moral "organized reflex" is irrational, indeed "infra-human" so to speak; in other words, insufficient to orient the subject toward human action properly so called. All those things that later on and even in adult life hinge upon this reflex and its attendant anxiety will be, in exact proportion to this dependence, inferior to the truly human level of objective knowledge of real values and their free choice.

As a corollary to this, what characterizes the superego in its essentially egocentric aspect is that it rests upon its *instinctive* fear of destruction or of suffering. One could remark in passing how deeply opposed such a reaction is to the self-sacrificing atti- tude of true Christian morality which is entirely founded upon relationship with others: on our rela- tions with God and with our neighbor, according to the words of Christ Himself.

Finally, then, toward the stage where the child, still more instinctual than reflective, starts upon his first experience of social relationships, in the phase known as the "oedipus" stage, this *pseudo-moral* reflex will be inclined to assume a new emotional coloration without at the same time losing the very primitive characteristics we have just described. This emo- tional coloring corresponds roughly to something that distantly resembles the feeling of guilt. Very briefly the adult of the same sex is resented as a sort of threatening judge in relation to whom the child has the tendency to experience some anxiety as though he were guilty of something that would bring about terrifying consequences. It is easy to see that this guilt is still emotional, egocentric and instinctive; that it resembles only vaguely and very remotely a true and developed sense of guilt, to which we shall return presently. It is still all wrapped up in the "fear for self" of threatening consequences — the primitive notion of sanctions—that one has oneself run the risk of provoking.

Formation of the Superego

Contrary to what we might think, the formation of the superego is not only one of the essential compo- nents of the basic psyche, but it is actually of the most primary importance to it. It is indeed upon this instinctive regulation of the impulses, always a little incoherent and often without references to any hier- archy of values, that the subject will later on build his own conscious and free moral dynamism.

To a certain extent it is a kind of call for the creation of a true moral sense at the level of the spirit. This emotional conflict will demand the development of a rational choice and, in order to be able clearly to debate the question of good and evil, it is necessary for the subject to begin by *sensing* the dilemma as a confused source of anxiety and as a stimulus toward launching his own real existence. In other words, the setting to work of a moral dynamism is got under way by this prefiguration, as yet entirely confused and instinctual, of the superego.

Obviously, however, the evolution of the subject must continue. Without method or calculation the child will, progressively and by stages, re-examine in some way by the light of reason the prohibiting reflexes that he has within him. He will begin to know the exterior world no longer as something that sets in motion these "introjected" reflexes, of which we have been speaking, but as a system of objective values requiring his deliberate choice.

A little reflection will show what a tremendous task this is. For these values are themselves related to one another and according to a hierarchy whose aspects we divine by a purely traditional knowledge (the "natural law"); but we cannot at the same time grasp their general tenor and their details unless we receive the ultimate and transcendent indications that can be given by God alone, the sovereign end. It is therefore both by the light of his reason and by the principles provided for him by Revelation and the Faith that the child is able to break one after the other the constricting reflexes of the superego and replace them by free, reflective and deliberate choices and by positive and dynamic attitudes of action. At least that is what should happen if he is to arrive at a real liberty of action corresponding to the maximum in metaphysical autonomy marking the human personality. Where this evolution is achieved to the fullest possible extent, the acts carried out by the subject are human acts in the maximum sense of the word with their full spiritual significance. To give only one example: having resolved the anxiety of the threat of punishment, the adolescent can then without insurmountable difficulties develop an attitude toward sexual behavior amounting to a lucid and positive practice of the virtue of chastity instead of wearing himself out in the struggle between his desire for balance and the attraction of the thing forbidden.

This work of replacement of an emotional pseudo-morality of the superego by the true morality of the spirit is never perfectly achieved, that is in the etymological sense of *accomplished* or *done*. (This is what St. Paul means by that remarkable sentence: "For I do not that good that I will"—Romans 7:15). It is a matter, then, of continuing the work patiently throughout life. Certain anxiety reflexes of childhood take tens of years to fall away, and even then only when help is given. We all need, some day or another, to go over many things, to revise in the light of Faith those so-called "values" which are not genuine at all, or at least are of merely secondary importance. How many adult Christians need badly to view things from this standpoint?

Such-and-such a very pious person, who tears her neighbors to pieces or lives in a blissful state of egoism would be seized by palpitations of the heart at the very idea of eating meat on a Friday when traveling. . . . This is moral caricature that directly contradicts the personal teaching of Christ: people are obsessed with an intense anxiety about some secondary precept, and so are prevented from living and understanding the major precept of charity. It would be desirable if the adult Christian had the courage and the clarity of vision to "pinpoint" such a pseudo-moral reflex in himself and to express it honestly on a piece of paper; then the following evening to bring it face to face with the true moral values as Christ taught them. Perhaps he then could assume or reject it according to whether or not this aspect of his behavior holds an important place. In other words, he could put it in its true place as an objective reference and no longer as an emotional and subjective reverberation.

The Superego and Reason

While the superego is a primary stage toward the later orientation of action and behavior, it is fraught, nevertheless, with danger. It can cease to be a preparatory step and can actually prove an obstacle in the evolution toward a conscious morality. This happens if the emotional intensity of the anxiety that constitutes part of it is so great that it is impervious to the rational activities of thought and reflection. In this case, indeed, it continues insurmountable and it is the superego that takes over the work that should be done by reason. Then instead of breaking out layer by layer and transforming itself into a new reality, the superego will, on the contrary, retract the higher faculties toward its own emotional blockage. The subject will then rationalize this anxiety, but in a manner still unconscious and reflexive so that he will justify by principles that are apparently quite reasonable an emotional twist he can neither surmount nor leave behind. Thus the normal transition, from "instinct to thought" will take place only apparently: the subject will still be governed by his unconscious superego encased in defensive mechanisms, that is to say, defended by this "infra-human" instinct. The superior powers, paradoxically, will then be returned to and taken into the service of infantile emotions that cannot be formulated.

From now onward the result is a false infantile "morality," a semi-superstitious morality, very emotional and therefore completely egocentric and of the legalistic type. Its "principles" will be very strict, narrow, of a kind most certain to maintain the existent anxiety or constraint and in itself all the more effective in its work of restriction since it is unconscious. The real concept of charity is now practically nonexistent, and the Christian terms will be used only as labels; they are indeed being simply "plagiarized." The whole psychological attitude is now becoming a kind of involuntary fraud: we are denoting as Christian a state of mind that is in fact nothing more nor less than a naturalistic and rationalist regression as far removed as it could be from the teaching and the morality of the Gospels. When this process takes place collectively — and nothing is more contagious than a constraint or an anxiety—it can produce groups of people who with the best faith in the word vehemently defend a doctrine that is more or less false, putting the accent on fear (fraudulently designated as the "fear of the Lord") and on an authority bearing a closer resemblance to Zeus or Woden than to the Mystery of the Most Holy Trinity revealed to us by Sacred Scripture. The transcendence of Almighty God, according to the Bible and according to the Church, is to be found in the sphere of love and not in the arbitrary dictatorship of some oriental tyrant. . . .

The danger of the superego lies in an overstrong emotional intensity in the course of its formation. In one way or another the child is brought up against constricting factors that are too threatening or too often repeated, and is not sufficiently helped to quiet down or to overcome the resulting emotions. While this mechanism, starting from a certain threshold of consciousness, is sometimes the generator of neurosis (scruples, phobias, neuroses of failure, and so on), it will more frequently provoke only slight contractions, small hindrances in the moral orientation, inadequacies of development, that will not have pathological repercussions upon the personality.

It is only too clear that the educative attitude of parents and others immediately surrounding the child plays the primary role in the formation of his superego. We shall not lay stress upon the gross mistakes that can be made by the use of mysterious threats that these people hope will keep a child quiet. Such a practice practically reaches the dimension of crime. Who can ever essay a guess at what irreparable damage has been set in motion in the psyche and the religious outlook of the child by threats of the "bogeyman"—when it is not—heaven help us!—the priest who "will come and take you away if you are not good. . . ." The perniciousness of such practices is too obvious for us to dwell upon it.

As always, it is the excesses on one side or the other that constitute the dangers from the educative standpoint.

A type of education that is too rigid and too authoritarian in character runs the risk, as anyone can easily see, of encouraging a constriction of the superego too intense for the child to escape from later on. This situation is unfortunately much too commonly found, particularly in certain countries where a special concept of the family prevails; this concept is too close to that of the primitive tribe, or the Roman "paterfamilias" in all its rigor, to be properly called Christian. The child in such an environment actually lives—whether this manifests itself or not—in a fundamental attitude of terror. This attitude will be complicated by the fact that, unconsciously sensing parental authority as absolute and totemic, the child of from eight to twelve years, then the adolescent and later even the adult man, will be unable to sustain on the unconscious emotional plane any challenge to the "principles" he has been taught; such a challenge would, in fact, appear to him more outrageous and dangerous than the risk of not applying these same "principles." An emotional confusion hereupon ensues which is a very different matter from the idea of sin. And since the father, in spite of everything, is still only an ordinary man like everyone else, the inevitable mistakes he must have made, even if in all good faith, cannot be calmly recognized and accepted as such by his son who is later on imprisoned in his emotional anxiety.

However, at the extreme opposite, paradoxical though it may appear, is the parental attitude that consists in "letting the child do whatever he takes a fancy to so that he won't develop complexes." This attitude is the ready generator of a superego quite as disproportionate, if not more so, and its educational value is no greater. The child's need for activity is necessarily exercised in an incoherent manner during his early years. If this activity is not guided, canalized, reasonably *oriented* by those around him the anxiety experienced by the child is perhaps even stronger in the face of the perpetually unknown, of the unexplorable ocean of liberty that confronts him. Consequently, the child will create his own disproportionately intense "ritual" defenses against the reality that must be dealt with. He passes through all his experiences as if he were weighed down by responsibilities he cannot assume and from which he takes refuge in cabalistic protective reflexes that may possibly paralyze his emotional development. Experience shows that children brought up according to this "system"—which is nothing more nor less than a defection on the part of their parents—remain actually as infantile in their adult life as those of the preceding type, despite an appearance of "liberty of action" that indeed only hides a permanent unconscious anxiety. They walk through their lives like blind people in unfamiliar surroundings.

Religious Concept of Sin

We spoke a little earlier of "sin." This again is a term that must be most carefully defined because it can become a pretext for regrettable confusions.

The concept of "sin," in fact, is not precisely a moral concept but a *religious* one. That is to say that sin does not mean "an act which is not in conformity with the law," but rather a disturbance of the relationship between the person who commits it and some other person. In other words, and to take precise definition to its extreme limit, we would say that "sin" is not the equivalent of "misconduct." In misconduct we see a breach of the principles, or a lack of "Good" abstractly conceived as an idea. In "sin" the same act takes on a completely different dimension: the "Good" is in fact recognized as Someone, in other words, not as an idea but as a living Person with whom a dialogue of love is taking place.

This distinction, which can never be sufficiently emphasized in normal teaching, is nevertheless fundamental: it differentiates between morality that is rationalist and legalistic (that is to say, a morality naturalistic in spirit) and Christian morality properly speaking. It enables us to conceive of human behavior not as a more or less fatalistic contest (ritualistic, too, according to the Pharisees) with a "law" that is purely arbitrary and totem-like in character, but as a personal relationship, a deepening of love of God, who first of all has loved us. It is at one and the same time the whole meaning of the Canticle of Canticles and the parable of the Prodigal Son.

From the psychological point of view this distinction is of the utmost importance: a "moral notion of misconduct" corresponds in fact to the unevolved stage of the superego; the moral notion of sin in the full religious sense corresponds, on the other hand, to the adult attitude—giving, relational, psychologically normal. The reflexes of the superego, as we have said, are instinctively egocentric: it is the exclusive risk to his own security that the subject perceives at this age, under the guise of an anxiety or constraint. The adult should normally have outgrown this egocentric attitude to a great extent, and be able to perceive the primordial necessity of communion with "the other," placing on this level the security of the Self and of the Other, desired in itself as the successful outcome of the fullness of living.

We here find again on the plane of purely natural psychology a correspondence to the teaching of Christ in the perspective of the supernatural: "Whoever shall lose his life shall find it." To truly find oneself one must renounce egocentrism from the roots and risk everything in a dynamic offering. This corresponds, too, to the absolute primacy of the "precept of love" emphasized vigorously by Christ on numerous occasions and which St. Thomas, among other doctors, was to develop within a very exhaustive philosophical framework: the Love of God and of our neighbor *for themselves*.

Outside of this dominant viewpoint it may be said that there is no authentic Christian morality. So obviously the psychological effects of the "bad action" run the risk of being profoundly misjudged.

At this point the usual vocabulary is again most bothersome. When, for instance, we speak of "guilt" we mean first of all the materiality of the deed: X is *guilty* of this action: this means that it was he who did it and that the act was bad. (This affirmation should not be confused, as people are often tempted to do, with another, namely: X is *responsible* for this action, which is a completely different problem.)

But this term "guilt" also designates the complex psychological effects (involving judgment, emotions, etc.) brought by his misconduct upon the person who has committed it. This is the *sentiment* or feeling of guilt. And here there is danger of the introduction of an equivocal note. If, in short, this sentiment is only an egocentric constriction in connection with the persistent superego, it will be felt and expressed by the word "guilt," but it will not correspond, despite religious appearances, to the *sense of sin*. In the fullness of the adult psychology and in a truly Christian perspective, sin will be felt not as a frightening or constraining threat, superstitiously feared because of its import for oneself, but as an attack on the Other, God and our neighbor, because we have not sufficiently *loved* them. And as we know from Revelation that God's Love for us is infinitely strong, at the very moment we recognize our need for pardon and so come to understand the "sense of sin" in its full Christian significance, it will become, instead of a paralyzing constraint, a singularly stimulating sorrow enabling us to deepen our life in relation to God, in other words, our spiritual life.

It is in this sense that St. Augustine propounds the apparent paradox: "Even sin is useful."

It is essential for parents and educators to have clearly in mind this distinction between the "feeling of guilt" which is a very loose and ambiguous idea (very easily confused with elements of the infantile unconscious) and the "sense of sin" as we have just defined it. Now, if it can be stated that the child of from four to five years of age has begun to perceive the idea of good and bad, can it be truly said that he is able to have a full concept of "sin," when he has not yet passed harmoniously through the stage of his first social experience—the "oedipus" conflict? And this is still only one discovery. The sense of the *personality* of the "Other" without which he cannot have a precise sense of sin will still require the crisis of adolescence in order to be developed further at the conscious level, and will go on maturing and deepening for the rest of his life.

The attitude of "penance" corresponds, moreover, to this deepening. And it offers this paradox: it is possible to be *at the same time* filled with grief and repentance for having betrayed someone (the tears of the Apostle Peter are a dramatic illustration of this) and yet profoundly steeped in sovereign hope.

This attitude, which is both a virtue and a gift of God, corresponds to a dynamism of *conversion* that grows more and more powerful. Here, too, is the essential role of the Sacrament of Penance, where man, recognizing his weakness, meets with God, whose strength saves him. It is, in one sense, the very opposite of the legalistic sentiment of guilt: its sense is outward and giving and no longer egocentric. Moreover, while the adult idea of real guilt (i.e., perception of the failure to love) can play a valid role in regard to other human beings, it remains despite everything only relative: in their fallibility or their bad will, analogous to our own, other people can themselves fail in love with respect to us; fundamentally daily life is only, at least in part, an exchange of bad dealings, intentional or involuntary. . . .

But with God it is a very different matter. He loves us *a priori*, if we may put it that way: and any defection is not conceivable in His absolutely gratuitous Love. The idea of betraying this Love, by revolt or by indifference, is monstrous. And when we realize that we have actually done this, the result is a kind of confusion or profound distress, of radical disquiet, that may be very distantly compared to the complex sentiment a man might feel when he realizes that he had gone so far as to wound his best friend or his beloved wife in a very sensitive matter.

Finally, the Christian attitude of penance is continuous: the state of human nature in temporal life is such that in spite of our own will we remain always below the level of the Love that would be an adequate response to the divine friendship and good will. This attitude of penance (i.e., "conversion") consists in recognizing very deeply this inadequacy, this flaw in our being, so that we may release ourselves by a continual spiritual effort, *calm and without anxiety,* from the excessive grip of our temporal condition. To realize every day a little more clearly the temporary and relative nature of our status and orient ourselves toward the real condition of the redeemed as it is offered and given us by God— such is, in brief, the "sense of sin," a religious reality much more than a "morality" of the mind.

Objectivity of Parental Sanctions

It is necessary, therefore, for the child, then the adolescent and later the young man and young woman, to be able progressively to discern, even beyond emotional reactions, the mysterious transcendence of the personal life of God, infinitely distinct from every human person who surrounds them and particularly distinct from parental authority, so fragile in itself and so subject to the weaknesses of the human nature of the parents.

This demands from the parents a genuine objectivity and clarity of outlook regarding their own limitations, in a word, a genuine humility. Once again it is a matter of the golden mean, of proper balance. A father who dares not assume his responsibilities or give orders because of an inverted pride that has become an excessive humility is just as baneful an influence on his child as the father who wishes his authority to be considered as absolute, infallible and beyond all possible discussion. The child who has a very keen sense of justice and does not yet know how to allow for gradations, has a tendency to consider his parents as ultimate authorities, at least during the early years of his life. If this tendency is encouraged and sustained by the parents through a mode of behavior that is more instinctive than reasoned, the day will come, perhaps all too soon, when the child will discover the weaknesses of these "ultimates" and a dramatic reaction will ensue in which there is a grave risk that the moral values will be obliterated. If, on the contrary, the child perceives that his parents are reasonable people who are *seeking* to be just, and who, therefore, logically recognize their mistakes, he will early develop an enhanced confidence in them; but above all he will have the increasing opportunity of discerning the existence of a living and absolute justice of a truly transcendent order. That is to say, God.

It is a daily experience: people have more confidence in a leader who knows how to shoulder his responsibilities and yet at the same time recognizes in the face of the evidence the mistakes he has made. His concern to be objective is a major element for the security of those who are under his orders; he is recognized as a human being, and people obey him without dispute for the very reason that he is accessible to discussion.

A little episode observed in the course of a journey will provide a useful example here. The scene took place at "coffee time" in a popular café in a provincial town. A family came in and settled around a table: father, mother, two children, one of whom was a little boy of seven or eight years of age. They ordered a lemonade for the little fellow and settled down to enjoy their refreshments, chatting to each other. The little fellow, enraptured with all that was going on in the café, kept turning and twisting around in his chair so as to miss nothing. Then a sudden movement caused him to knock over his glass and

spill the lemonade all over the table. A quick slap
from his mother. Floods of tears. Then a couple of
seconds later the mother leaned over toward him and
said: "I am sorry, dear. I shouldn't have slapped
you. You didn't do it on purpose." Undoubtedly it
would have been much better if the child had never
received the ill-timed slap: but once the thing was
done, there was no better educational attitude than
the one the mother adopted. The little fellow's look,
his smile and the kiss he gave her spoke volumes;
and this fleeting moment, undoubtedly showing the
mother's fundamental attitude, opened all possible
doors to a true moral conscience.

How many times do parents, although very well
intentioned, compromise a later moral evolution by
interjecting values that have nothing to do with a
situation: "If you are not good you will hurt Baby
Jesus. . . ." A monstrous lie: this will hurt Daddy
or Mama, perhaps, but "Baby Jesus" has nothing at
all to do with the question. Surely it can already be
of enough importance without directly implicating the
suffering Christ for the child to learn to make an
effort not to hurt a human being; quite simply, in
other words, to exercise a still embryonic charity that
is generously and duly considerate of the existence
of "another."

Moreover, it would be good for the parents to
make the effort to achieve adequate objectivity in the
choice and application of the sanctions that are
sometimes necessary. In other words, they should
attempt to estimate the opportuneness and the importance of the sanction in the *interior world of the
child* as against the fault he has committed. If he
has not realized that it was a fault, why punish him?
And if he has not realized the importance of the fault
in adult eyes, why make the punishment severe?
Again an example will make this easier to understand. Let us imagine a drawing room with a grand

piano; across the piano lies a shawl of glowing irides-
cent colors and on the shawl there stands a precious
vase, a unique piece, in Chinese porcelain. Along
comes a little toddler of four years of age. He has
been forbidden to touch this shawl, but it tempts him
in spite of the warning. Indeed he has forgotten the
warning completely now because the shawl has been
left treacherously hanging within his grasp. He plays
with the shawl: he pulls it down; the vase shakes,
falls and breaks. Will the slap that immediately follows—if not indeed the spanking—really be connected with the guilt of the child or with the
subjective chagrin of the mother, a chagrin propor-
portionate to the value of the vase that she can no
longer display for her friends' admiration, not without a delicious touch of satisfaction when she observes their envy?

And so life goes on. And it is in details of this
kind that parents too frequently accumulate those
little mistakes that are liable to hinder a positive and
harmonious expansion of the moral conscience and
the "sense of sin."

Primitive Fear and Penance

For the religious evolution to be properly made
from the standpoint of the formation of the moral
conscience, then, it is necessary for the child to be
able to pass satisfactorily from the instinctive reflex
of primitive fear to the spiritual attitude of penance.
In other words, the occasions for him to crystallize
and "fix" his first anxiety or repression should be
reduced to a minimum.

In a normal atmosphere this part of the educational
task is not at all insurmountable even though the
occasions between birth and eight years of age for
receiving intense and repeated emotional shocks are
frequent indeed. But in a normal atmosphere, the

feeling of security experienced by the child of a united and fully adjusted family offsets in large measure the shocks to the emotions. The efforts of the parents to preserve unity are, as we have already said, of the very first importance. The truly Christian spirituality of Faith, Charity and Hope in the moral sense—where the "desire for Heaven" prevails over the "fear of Hell," where the love of God prevails over the fear of His punishment—contributes almost as much. It is very obvious that the reign of terror ("neurosis-provoking" according to the language of the psychologists) is at the opposite extreme from Christian thinking.

It may be of use to provide a few examples of genuine situations occurring in childhood that are particularly likely to bring about the crystallization or fixation of an anxiety or constriction. It is impossible to describe in detail all the situations that could arise, as it will be readily understood that this would involve an attempt to define the indefinite. Moreover, dynamic psychology is the study of individual and personal problems and if one were to try to extract from it certain general lines of direction one would simply be reducing it to the arbitrary and abstract level of a study of anonymous "cases." In the following pages, therefore, we have given examples taken from a group of many possible choices and selected them simply to clarify our thesis.

The first child is born to a couple in the early years of their married life. He is immediately the central object of general attention; he demands constant care; he incorporates a whole world of hopes. In addition to the continual attention of his mother everyone else around him is trying to see who can make him laugh, play, walk, talk and so on. He is, in short, the center of the world, and inevitably, in his own quite normal egocentrism, his "primary narcissistic stage" according to the technical expression, he senses himself as such from the time when he begins in a confused way to distinguish those around him. Quite suddenly, when he reaches the age of two, he discovers in a new cot another crying baby around whom everyone is dancing attendance just as they had done with him up to then. His "surprise" [1] is already tinged with a slight amount of anxiety: he is now obliged to share, he is no longer the *only* center of the world. Could he have "lost his value" since they have decided to bring along another baby? This *instinctive* emotion of frustration provokes an *instinctive* reflex toward "recovery" that may be expressed in a thousand ways. The child will try to make people concern themselves with him; he will insist on being carried; he will stop making any progress in talking; he will wet his bed. In short, he will "play the little baby" in order to recover a type of affection this other has taken from him.

When the anxiety is very intense, which may be for a variety of imponderable or accidental reasons, and according to the unconscious taking root of the instinct of aggression, this desire to recover a lost affection could go even so far as a "wish to see the end of" the intruder, the "thief of love." Though timidly, to be sure, the child may even manifest this wish by making crude gestures of "destruction" or "elimination." If the family atmosphere is such that this anxiety is calmed or exorcised, if, in other words, the child is brought to "accept" the newborn baby as a brother after having instinctively regarded him as a rival, everything will turn out well. (The frequency of enuresis in children—when not due to

---

[1] All the time, in default of an adequate vocabulary, we are using terms of adult psychology, and the better to indicate their analogous character we have put them in quotation marks.

physical causes, of course—shows clearly that quite often scars remain in the unconscious of the subject.) But if there are many circumstances working against the child such as ill-controlled irritation on the mother's part, and later on pejorative comparisons with the younger child "who is far better behaved than you" (we will not even mention here the people who demonstrate preferences)—if all these factors come into play, the anxiety will become deeply rooted instead of being dissolved. The child continues to react in the same way as at the start—"has he lost his value?" By means of the first punishments drawn down on him by his reflexes of "recovery" the way is then rapidly cleared for the "guilt" of the superego. Is he "to blame"? Is he "guilty" by reason of his very existence and without even knowing why? This guilt anxiety or constriction, very easily and very frequently linked to the anxiety of inferiority or of "self-devaluation," is in great danger later on of misleading the moral sense and hindering an expansion in the giving stage. Scrupulosity follows: an anxious craving for perfectionism; instinctive need for "rites" to exorcise this unconscious constraint—all this strongly endangers the balance of the religious sentiment, above all when the Sacraments such as Penance are invested by the child with this character of "ritualistic phobia."

Moreover, this emotional contraction, as a result of an inferiority anxiety, runs the risk of bringing in reflexes of "super-compensation," according to the technical term, that are in direct opposition to the religious, spiritual attitude. This can create real and serious barriers against the subject's later approach to a Christian view of the world and of his destiny. The reflex of super-compensation is often expressed by an anxiety for perfection, an "advance scruple" which is nothing more than an infantile and egocentric desire for the absolute. The subject does everything and reacts to everything as if he were being driven by an instinctive need for recognition as absolute in his own worth. The most elementary good sense will show this as an emotional difficulty of some importance, since the first requisite for entering upon a proper relationship with God is to realize that it is He who is the absolute and not we, who are dependent, limited and relative. In other words, this unconscious psychic reflex is analogous on its "sub-moral" plane to the spiritual attitude that constitutes pride. This reflex acts as an underlying and sometimes extremely constraining contra-dynamism in the religious education of the child and later on in the personal thinking of the adolescent and the adult. For such subjects an education that is purely moralistic instead of being a progressive introduction to love gravely risks "blocking" the religious sentiment forever at the level of an insurmountable emotional contradiction. This is something which, unfortunately, happens all too often.

In a few words, after this somewhat lengthily explained example, we shall touch on two other possible contractions in connection with the stage known as "oedipean."

It can happen that the sentiment of frustration experienced by the child is dominant or particularly intense, or that fortuitous circumstances (leaving aside a bad family atmosphere) may prevent the normal transition from this first "oedipus" phase. Reflexes of recovery, still instinctive, could take root, sometimes with curious resurgences of the primitive, alimentary stage. The child will compensate for his unconscious emotional void by little pilferings of food or of money—thefts which are in short symbolical. The very profound emotional nature of such behavior will naturally impede him from admitting or recognizing it, the more so as *he does not know* why he behaves as he does. Besides, he has as yet no objective idea of the value of what he is stealing —the exact knowledge of what a five-dollar bill represents, for example, is not inborn. All this runs the danger of gravely complicating the education and opening up of a moral relational sense that is authenticly Christian.

Along a very different line there could develop in the child a compulsive urge for success and for autonomy which, as an adult man or woman will prohibit him, partly unconsciously, from acceding to his full liberty for fear of some arbitrary and unknown "punishment." With the boy, for example, the "oedipus rivalry" may provoke this constraint: the child can resent his rival as a threat, that might be expressed analogically in this way: "If I claim to supplant my father, or to put myself on a level with him, he will (or 'someone' will) suppress my masculinity, the thing giving the initial force to my ego." It is useless to repeat that this expresses in all too clear terms realities that are infinitely confused in spite of their intensity. The masculinity of which he is emotionally conscious is symbolized for the child by his distinct sexual anatomy. That is the reason why this anxiety is known in technical language as the "castration anxiety." If it becomes fixed it may also bring along later a kind of unconscious cultivation of failure, an incapacity for becoming positively involved in life. But, above all, it may cause this failure to be felt as fatal, insurmountable and totally destructive. This will hardly help the subject toward the lofty idea of an accepted failure as a fruitful experience, a condition for divine victory in which he can participate through Grace. This is the exact Christian idea of suffering and of death, the pivot of the religious attitude.

The Age of Reason

To round off what is concerned with the progressive formation of the moral conscience, it seems necessary to make a few reflections on what is currently known as "the age of reason."

If some attention is paid to modern psychology, it will quickly be apparent that this age is fairly variable. But above all, one is induced to specify a distinction that is a little unusual.

If the question arises as to when the child perceives in a conscious manner the idea of good and evil in such a way that this idea to a certain extent conditions and motivates his personal choice, one could think that he arrives at this threshold at the time of the "latent period," that is to say, at the moment when the "emotional fermentation" of the first years gives place to the development of the superior and rational faculties of the spirit. The transition is always progressive; therefore it is highly artificial to endeavor to fix it at a typical age. This age varies imperceptibly with different subjects, and even if one can establish by certain signs that the transition has been made, it is in reality quite impossible to state exactly at what precise moment it began. It is a question of an expanding dynamism; and its potentiality, the thing which makes up the human being in his specific nature, is not comparable to a sudden mutation. In a very general manner one might say that toward the age of seven, unless there have been anomalies or backwardness, the transition to the age of reason is verifiable.

But the fact remains that the "good" and the "evil" are strongly sensed as "good for me" or "bad for me." That is to say, that the emotional forms, so to speak, in which this knowledge of good and of evil is exercised at the outset, are still normally very strongly egocentric and very slightly relational. More-

over, the instinctive powers have passed only the
early stages of their development and are, to a certain extent, still sleeping. The subject has not yet
realized their full manifestations. From the point of
view of aggression as much as of sex, the child is as
yet living on only confused impulses, more or less
embryonic.

The crisis of adolescence is needed before the
transcendance of the giving and serving stage required
for adult maturity is consciously perceived and consciously experienced—before, in other words, the
"good" and the "evil" are recognized as being "in
oneself" and as "personal." (It is remarkable to
note that the spirit of evil, regressive pride is presented in Judeo-Christian Revelation as a "created"
person who refused relationship with the person of
the Creator.) But this crisis is also needed in order
that the subject may experience his definitive forces
at the level of instinct and may recognize them—
in order, in other words, for him to attain a sufficient
level of conscious knowledge of himself and of liberty.

In this respect it is quite remarkable to read in
the *Summa* of St. Thomas Aquinas (IIa, IIae, Q.189,
art. 5) his short reflection upon the value of vows
and of children's entry into the religious life. The
vow of simple promise made to God, he says, can
be impeded in children "by lack of the liberty of
decision; this happens in the case of children who
have not yet sufficient use of reason as a result of
which they are susceptible to fraud. Such use of
reason children attain most often toward the age of
fourteen — girls toward the age of twelve — years
which are called 'years of puberty.' With certain
children it is earlier when they reach it, with others
it is later, according to the different dispositions of
nature."

Here is food for reflection, for what St. Thomas
says corresponds with the scientific findings of mod-

ern psychology. Is there not sometimes a too great tendency to expect or to demand of children a moral effort along lines they are not yet ready to adopt? Before puberty, says St. Thomas, the child has not customarily sufficient use of his reason (that is, of his spiritual faculties) to subscribe to a way of life that is free. In his educational demands does the adult always take this elementary truth into account? Is there not rather a tendency to confuse "the age when reason awakens" with the "age of free choice"?

And modern psychology superabundantly demonstrates that if education mistakes the considerable difference between these two "ages," if it overburdens the still fragile emotional life of the child of prepuberty age with demands of an adult type, a delay in psychological evolution is inevitably caused and the mind is impeded in its upward motion toward the adult moral age of liberty. Such is, in brief, the significance of the superego reinforced by an education that is purely moralist and not *religious,* so that it is made more or less impervious to the illumination of "reason," according to the language of St. Thomas, that is to say, impervious to the illumination of the Holy Spirit.

VI
Morality
and
Religion

THE preceding chapter dealing with the psychological foundations and genesis of the moral conscience brings us back to an important point: the real relationship between this moral conscience and the religious sentiment. Confusion between the two is indeed very easy and inevitably runs the risk of generating, though they may be disguised by a surface religious terminology, an attitude and a way of living that are in fact no more than legalistic. Moreover, there is nothing surprising in this, since the genuine religious attitude means a continual transcending of the natural order and of the sentient and rational world. Such an attitude is not easy because, if one might dare to put it that way, it consists in being torn between the attraction of the supernatural and the logical and spontaneous inclination toward realities that can be immediately perceived. The danger of the latter predominating has been continuous throughout religious history. In its most characteristic form it was manifested, for example, in the mentality of the Pharisees. Their observance of rites, their satisfaction with having fulfilled "precepts," their preoccupation with the law, recognized as a limiting entity, their major concern for exterior and conventional behavior, all these led inexorably to the complacency of mind and duplicity of action so violently denounced by Christ.

If one desires to orient religious education in its true sense it is obviously essential that those whose work this will be, parents and educators, should themselves possess to the highest degree, a conscious and reflective attitude, a *religious* attitude and not a merely moralistic outlook. If the modern psychology of dynamisms protests in the name of mental hygiene against narrow legalism — as is shown in recently published works—it does not, by any means, raise objections to a true religious attitude which, far from working against natural dynamisms, tends, on the contrary, to expand them beyond their ordinary limits into a positive morality.

The purpose of religious education is to open for the child all possible means of access to the Faith in Christ. It is therefore indispensable that educators should know as clearly as they possibly can in what this Faith consists, so that they will not direct the child up some blind alley along which they themselves have perhaps gone astray. In the religious order of things, in fact, it is Faith that dominates life and not the other way around.

Three Characteristics of Faith

The first characteristic of Faith is for it to be objective. That is to say, it has nothing to do with "impressions" or "opinions." It is a relationship born of knowledge with "something" quite other than the interior world of the subject. It rests essentially upon the independent existence of this "something" which is *a priori* whether we have knowledge of it or not.

The second characteristic of Faith consists in this, that the "something" is in fact *Someone*. Contrary to the habitual formula, we do not believe "verities" which are abstract ideas or principles; we believe *in Someone* who is God, who is Christ, who is the Church, the Mystical Body of Christ. This is not an intellectual choice, nor a philosophical conviction, but the consent to a relationship with a living person. It is quite evident that the power necessary to attain to the possibility of this dialogue with the Absolute Transcendence infinitely exceeds the potentialities of our created nature. It is in itself the mysterious gift of this transcendence.

The third characteristic of Faith is that this *Someone* has taken a real place in the history of the human race, and that He has given His message through and by means of the story of a people, using our language to speak to us either Himself or through an interpreter. From that point on the Faith is transmitted by what we might almost call the contagion or contact of testimony. The comparison takes on greater significance with the extension of human relations. Those who knew the historical Christ during His life on earth and after His Resurrection have made Him known to the world. And each one of us enters into relationship with Him in the *chiaroscuro* of Faith. It is this existential dimension that is the first factor of religious "contagion"; in fact it is what gives vigor and dynamism to those things that can be said and preached of the Christian Mystery. Religious education cannot be conceived of except in this way; it cannot be compared with the teaching of any branch of knowledge, no matter how important it may be. Again it is necessary for educators—we should be tempted to call them "instructors"—clearly to perceive the unique and specifically *religious* nature of their task.

Religius Nature of Education

The central text from this point of view, around which all Christian religious thought is crystallized, is in a very strange passage in St. Paul's Epistle to the Romans (7:1-25):

"Know you not, brethren (for I speak to them that know the law), that the law hath dominion over a man, as long as it liveth? . . .

"Therefore, my brethren, you also are become dead to the law, by the body of Christ; that you may belong to another, who is risen again from the dead, that we may bring forth fruit to God.

"For when we were in the flesh, the passions of sins, which were by the law, did work in our members, to bring forth fruit unto death.

"But now we are loosed from the law of death, wherein we were detained; so that we should serve in newness of spirit, and not in the oldness of the letter.

"What shall we say, then? Is the law sin? God forbid! But I do not know sin, but by the law; for I had not known concupiscence, if the law did not say: *Thou shalt not covet.*

"But sin, taking occasion by the commandment, wrought in me all manner of concupiscence. For without the law sin was dead.

"And I lived some time without the law. But when the commandment, sin revived,

"And I died. And the commandment that was ordained to life, the same was found to be unto death to me.

"For sin, taking occasion by the commandment, seduced me, and by it killed *me.*

"Wherefore the law indeed is holy, and the commandment holy, and just, and good.

"Was that then which is good, made death unto

me? God forbid! But sin, that it may appear sin, by that which is good, wrought death in me; that sin, by the commandment, might become sinful above measure.

"For we know that the law is spiritual; but I am carnal, sold under sin.

"For that which I work, I understand not. For I do not that good which I will; but the evil which I hate, that I do.

"If then I do that which I will not, I consent to the law, that it is good.

"Now then it is no more I that do it, but sin that dwelleth in me.

"For I know that there dwelleth not in me, that is to say, in my flesh, that which is good. For to will is present with me; but to accomplish that which is good, I find not.

"For the good which I will, I do not; but the evil which I will not, that I do.

"Now if I do that which I will not, it is no more I that do it, but sin that dwelleth in me.

"I find then a law, that when I have a will to do good, evil is present with me.

"For I am delighted with the law of God, according to the inward man:

"But I see another law in my members, fighting against the law of my mind, and captivating me in the law of sin, that is in my members.

"Unhappy man that I am, who shall deliver me from the body of this death?

"The grace of God, by Jesus Christ our Lord. Therefore, I myself with the mind serve the law of God; but with the flesh, the law of sin."

This long description of the fundamental contradiction in man torn between his love of the good and his oppression by the law leads St. Paul to explain vigorously that salvation is essentially found in faith in Christ Jesus, crucified and risen from the dead, who delivers us from slavery. It is not obedience to the Law that saves us since, on the contrary, the attempt we make to obey it only further emphasizes our own powerlessness. It is the grace, the love, the mercy of God in the Person of Christ, to whom we give the adhesion of our Faith, freed at last from all constraint.

Without straining after a paradox we might say that the very essence of the Christian outlook rests in a profound perception not of the futility but of the inadequacy of the mere observance of precepts.

According to St. Paul's teaching human history may be summarized thus: before the law had been given (knowledge of the "natural law" and the instructions given to Moses including the Ten Commandments) man lived in ignorance and illusion. The law reveals man to himself as a divided being, struggling without hope. That is the idea of the law as a "pedagogue" that we again find in the Epistle to the Galatians, 3:24. The regime of the law cannot save him, for the letter kills. And only the experience of this death can make him accessible to the grace which comes to resolve his anxiety. From then on, through his faith in Christ, man is no longer a slave of the law; instead, he has a personal relationship of love and salvation with God who made the law to help man to understand his wretched position.

Such is the Christian's position: overwhelmed by the law, in a state of perpetual tension between his "will" and the "law of sin that is in his members" (Romans 7:23) he is saved in and through faith in Christ Jesus. His outlook on the law will never again be the same; he will look upon it, if one may dare so to express it, from the height of a friendship that has been re-established by the grace of God. He will be attached with his whole heart to this Living Person who has saved him, and he will endeavor to express his total loyalty to Him by the practical way he lives, and by his effort to observe the law which he now knows as the expression of Him who loves mankind. (Faith without good works, at the other extreme, is a still worse illusion, says St. James.) But the law will never again frighten the Christian; his efforts to observe it will be a consequence of his grateful love for God who loves him to the extent of becoming man and sacrificing His human life for him.

In the Christian perspective the *religious* conditions the moral. This is an essential and crucial truth whose emphasis is too often overlooked, yet it is of capital importance for practical living, and most particularly so for education. Just as preoccupation with the legalistic is the originator of psychopathological troubles so attention to the religious composes, restores and stimulates. In the anxious search for an impossible and frightening perfection the consciousness runs the risk of being thrown back in a sterile recession upon self. Whereas in the acceptance of mystery, in the opening up of our hearts to the transcendent salvation bestowed upon us by the Love of God, the positive dynamism of our response to this Love, though weakened by our impotence and finiteness, can only endeavor joyfully and peacefully to express by actions that are the existential and practical signs of our inarticulate love. This is the perpetual "Pharisaic-Christian" dialectic that we can follow easily through the long history of the Jewish people, many centuries even before Christ.

At every turn in the Old Testament we can see the prophets and the psalmists vigorously counteracting the perpetually reappearing excesses of ritualism, of formalism and of legalism. Rites and observances are nothing unless they express the *religion of the heart*. We must adore God, says Christ, "in spirit and in truth" and not only in gestures that have no substance in themselves. The "Miserere" psalm admirably sums up this spiritual approach. "With burnt offerings thou wilt not be delighted . . . a contrite and humbled heart, O God, thou wilt not despise" (Psalm 50). God in His Love asks for adherence to Love; without this living source all rites and gestures, all observances of the law are sterile, empty, ridiculous and productive only of death. The Pharisees are the "whited sepulchers." If in the course of His temporal life Christ showed an inexhaustible tenderness for the Samaritan, the woman who was a sinner, the woman taken in adultery, the publicans, there are two categories of people for whom His severity makes us tremble: the rich and the Pharisees. These two categories invited His wrath for they represented one and the same attitude: a blinding satisfaction with temporal success, whether financial or spiritual. The first condition of our responding to the God who redeems us is obviously not to close our eyes to this fact: by ourselves we are lost, incapable of resolving our anxieties, in a state of perpetual and terrible inadequacy before the Love of God, trembling in "sin." It is part of our human condition that we are sinners; and it is quite indispensable that we should know it and accept it *both* in despair *and* in hope. Thus we shall participate fully in the triumph of Christ and allow ourselves to be permeated by the omnipotence of His Love, concretely evident in human history. Is there a more subtle or more blinding obstacle than the legalistic illusion?

Now Christ declared plainly that He did not come to abolish the law, that not a comma of it would be changed. He came to *fulfill* it, because He alone, the Word, the Son of God, had sufficient power to return the unappreciated Love of the Father, incorporating us into Himself. The law, therefore, remains valid. But instead of being the "magic" and demoralizing principle of our powerlessness it becomes in its proper perspective the groundwork of our inarticulate attempts at love.

Insofar as the central presence of the living Mystery is not the very source of our thought and of our actions, we can speak undoubtedly of a "moral" education, but not of a religious education, and still less of a *Christian* education, whatever other terms we may employ.

Religious Education and Legalism

We consider it absolutely necessary to insist upon this point, because all too often in both modern teaching and in the contemporary outlook Christianity is confused with simple morality. Even the very rhythms of the religious life, the regular frequentation of the Sacraments, are presented exclusively as a kind of administrative and obligatory rule of procedure. There is a way of imparting the positive instructions of the Church that is curiously akin to the regulations of the Pharisees, and that sometimes goes so far as to be comparable to the minutiae laid down by the rabbis regarding work on the Sabbath. The routine insertion of such details into instruction ends by gravely falsifying religious education. On the one hand, it is directly opposed to the message of our Saviour; on the other it complicates the psychological evolution, strengthening the superego and making it more or less impervious to the light of the spirit. We should not forget that for the child up to eight years of age at least it is a question of a kind of emotional response to the emotional atmosphere that surrounds him—either by "direct assimilation" or by an attitude of reaction or opposition if the situation for one reason or another is intolerable. How often do we see young people violently rejecting "religion" by a defensive reaction against the insupportable caricature that has always been presented to them? What is serious is that this concept which has been engrained in their emotional substructure is quite preposterous, and later on there will be the greatest difficulty in trying to make them understand that *it is only a caricature.* All the subconscious reflexes of false guilt rise up against what they will regard as a contrived attempt to undo the harm done; for this attempt must consist in removing the parents from the pedestal that had raised them to the rank of totems or demigods. . . .

Religious education therefore requires that the family atmosphere, besides the minimum of balance and unity of which we have already spoken, be really religious and not solely preoccupied with laws that must be observed.

In the Christian perspective the behavior of man is a *personal* and free response to the call of God. The deliberate and considered orientation of this behavior, what is called its morality, is the *consequence* of a realized personal relationship with *Someone* who freely gives His creative and redeeming Love. The moral law was made to *guide* this deliberate orientation. Its value is purely *relative;* it is both the means of our realizing our fall from grace and the framework within which we may seek to respond to the Love of God. By itself and in itself it is nothing; abstract Good does not exist: it exists only in the Living God inscribed in the history of man in the Person of the Word made flesh.

In this perspective, as Christ repeated continually in His message, there exists but one normative instruction, one absolute precept, namely THOU SHALT LOVE. All the rest is only a consequence of this: on this "dependeth the whole law." The merest aspect of moral behavior is but a demand of Love: of God *and* of our neighbor, since these are inseparable. If this aspect of man's behavior is not explicitly and completely experienced and explained as such, it has not yet attained to the truly religious Christian level.

It is useless to multiply examples. To love one's neighbor is to wish him well; and this positive wish is so strong that we cannot agree to do him any harm or to prevent him from getting what is his due. The negative precepts have to do only with those things that are incompatible with the sovereign preoccupation of Charity. All *sin*, whatever it is, is a refusal of the Other, a flaw in the texture of Love, a closing in upon oneself. If it is not conceived as such, it is no longer "sin" but an infraction of the "law," and this attitude is no longer really religious or Christian.

From this point of view the study of the moral teaching of a St. Thomas of Aquinas, for example, is surprising. It is a morality of dynamism, or oriented energy, of return toward God. It is the morality of the journey toward beatitude, that is to say toward the dialogue of Love with God.

Here morality is given its true place, not as some abstract principle, but as the logical and limitless requirement of a life lived in relationship with Absolute Love.

Once this relationship is established, we are a long way from the legalistic routine and the rationalistic contagion that carry the subtle danger of falsifying the Christian mentality. In this perspective, which is properly speaking *religious*, we would even go so far as to say that the idea of "duty" as it is implicitly understood in the modern world is not adequate because it is insufficient.

The Christian concept of action is essentially positive and dynamic, and one cannot speak of negative virtue, which would consist in "not doing" this or that. Such a prohibition may be the logical consequence of a spiritual decision *to do* the opposite of a certain thing; in this case, if the choice is motivated by charity, the prohibition is perceived as evidence

of this but in itself has no essential interest. Virtue
does not reside in the attitude of concentrating on a
particular prohibition so that it will not be infringed;
it resides in the choice of good manifested by charity.
If I take the train to go from Paris to Deauville
what actually sets me in motion, the dynamism directing my activities, is the urge "to go to Deauville"
and not merely the desire "not to remain in Paris."
If such is not the case, then the action is either pathological or incoherent.

A relationship with our neighbor and with God
that is positive and experienced in the ever-deepening
search for communion—that is Christian morality. It
is essentially an ethic of Love. In other words, it is
neither a morality of "duty" nor of "acts," but a
morality of tendencies, or to put it even more precisely, a morality of personal powers, of virtues,
inspired by Love.

The "lists of sins" issued by the old penitentiaries
of the Middle Ages and to which present-day instruction is too often restricted are not without their uses:
such an enumeration of sinful actions can sometimes
serve to enlighten us, to inform us, to guide us. But
they become literally an obstacle, both from the psychological and the spiritual point of view, if they
are not explicitly and continually related to their
religious source, namely to a dynamic theology of
charity and all the virtues.

Experience that is both psychopathological and
spiritual clearly shows that a legalistic atmosphere
which puts the child on the wrong track since it mas-
querades under the appearance of Christian behavior
is one of the worst for his religious evolution.

One of the most profound and subtle causes of
the indisputable de-Christianization of the contemporary world that has become so dramatically apparent
seems to be this equivocation of a "Kantian" moralism being taken for Christian morality. This equivo-

cation masks and camouflages in a certain way the essential mystery of man as it is so vividly summed up in the verse we have quoted from the Epistle to the Romans. The man and woman "of duty" who are more or less put forward as the ideal are following a line that is more stoical—or at best patriarchal— than one that is truly Christian. It is not surprising, therefore, that such people should be very bad educators on both the natural and on the religious plane.

VII

Evolution of the
Religious Sentiment

THE harmonious development of religious life in the adult is, as we have seen, conditioned to a certain extent and as far as its "points of departure" are concerned, by the atmosphere in which he has lived in his childhood years. This conditioning is essentially emotional, long before it can be intellectual. Before instruction proper can begin, or even in the course of the elementary stages of this instruction, the emotional responsiveness of the child is what matters, and what will prepare him in a real and, we might say, tangible environment, for the later acceptance of the mystery of life.

To specify precisely all the elements of this emotional conditioning is impossible. The realities governing every life are too fluid, too dynamic, to be enclosed within the strict boundaries of a system, for this is precisely to destroy their existential character. Every individual has his own history; and each life commences all over again, with complete unpredictability and fundamental newness, the dialogue that is established between God and this individual through the intermediary of the Church.

Yet some problems of this evolution should be singled out for attention. They are certain psychological phenomena not customarily considered but which careful observation shows to be of the first importance, and which are clearly dangerous if consistently misunderstood.

Certain ways of presenting to the child the "face of God"—if we dare to use this expression—run the risk of confusing his evolution or of diverting it onto a wrong path. If, instead of using the stepping stones of the child's emotional life, education misjudges or destroys them, the religious edifice erected has many chances of being artificial, stereotyped and as inadequate for genuine psychological adjustment as for the reception of objective Revelation. It should not be forgotten that these stepping stones have been placed there by the Creator Himself. He does not contradict Himself in His work, and the findings of modern psychology bear further proof of that, for they demonstrate at just what point the Christian message responds, in a dimension surpassing the limits of created nature, to the actual needs of this very nature.

Religious education therefore should take very objectively into account these emotional elements, in order to enlighten the child regarding the divine mysteries in a gradual and continuous way that will be acceptable to him. At the same time it must progressively surmount and satisfy the instinctive need for imaginative and sensitive fulfillment that dwells so deeply in him. Thus he will be open to receive the personal action of God—which is called grace—whose essential work it is to enlarge to infinite dimensions through faith the faculties of knowledge and of love.

Paternal Image in Religious Teaching

A primary line of thought concerns the role of the emotional relations of the child with his parents in the first approaches to religious teaching.

It is one of the natural components of the religious sentiment in man that the divinity is represented under the symbol of an authoritarian "super-power." All the mythologies bear testimony to this, in the same way as they bear the mark, or at least the traces, of a sort of terror before this "super-power" which, or whom it is necessary to placate by various sacrifices, generally of a bloody nature, when its anger has been aroused. It is worth noting, too, that it was on the basis of a natural religious attitude of this kind that the Judeo-Christian Revelation began its work: one finds certain passages in the Bible that reproduce this primitive outlook to such a point that some people can hardly see beyond this, which precisely is not the positive meaning of the Word of God.

In the habitual Christian environment one of the first names the child grasps in connection with God is that of "Father." The sign of the cross and the "Our Father" are the usual means by which he learns this, since they are among the very first religious words and actions taught him. Yet for him this word "Father" does not convey a clear idea upon which his powers of reflection can work. As yet it corresponds only to a collection of emotional reactions toward a fatherly person whom he sees, or rather knows, to be at hand. Already, at a very early age, he tends toward the idealization of this fatherly person, since he is told that God is someone else, someone greater and more powerful. But this idealization comes about, if we may put it thus, from the starting point of the paternal image.

Collective depth psychology shows us that there exist certain universal archetypes according to which this process of development takes place. This is Jung's contribution and it is by no means a negligible one. The two archetypes most commonly found are the *sun* and the *king*. They are to be found in the unconscious of the adult, in particular in the course of dreams. But they are also to be found in the mythological religions, which readily turn on such themes. They occur, too, in the Judeo-Christian Revelation: Jehovah is compared with the sun, Christ is King. But this is only a point of departure for a progressive elaboration of the idea of the divine that reaches a degree to which human psychology, depending upon its own resources alone, cannot attain. For the boundary of this elaboration is an absolutely transcendent idea, even though it is rooted in the human and profoundly mysterious experience of love. The affirmation that God is in Himself the trinitarian unity of Three distinct Persons, equal, absolutely One and absolutely Three, breaks the bounds of all possible words to express this Mystery. But it leads to a foreshadowing of the knowledge that God is the transcendent Mystery of love, and it obliges man to break away from all the superstitions of the *sun* or the *king*, or in other words from all archetypes purely emotional in basis. These archetypes, in biblical language, for example, are only symbols and recognized as such, intended to express in some fashion an inexpressible reality.

It might almost be said, in a sense, that the affirmation of the Mystery of the Holy Trinity is the culmination of what God can teach us about Himself. It brings us to the threshold of the purely incomprehensible, opening it before us so that we may enter in. From now on we are very far beyond paternal images although they have served their purpose as a point of departure. Such progression toward the absolute transcendence, deeply rooted again in an actual experience, cannot be explained by a simple psychological process; this would be altogether insufficient as is shown by the study of the diverse non-Christian religions.

The vital thing, then, in the religious education of the child, is to do the utmost to help this potential progression, or at the very least to ensure that the child is not engulfed at the start by a kind of in-

ability to break away—as indeed he must do—from
the paternal image.

Children always have a tendency to regard adults,
and chiefly their parents, as absolutes. They depend
upon them for all their security and all their happiness. The father is the point of ultimate reference in
their instinctive system of values. "It is true because
Daddy said so" is a phrase very common in the
mouth of the little boy of four or five years of age;
and it is a phrase fraught with the possibility of
subsequent confusion. In fact, of course, the father
is only a man like all the rest, just as the little boy
will one day be himself. That is to say, the father is
a fallible human being, divided in himself, a sinner
and almost as unarmed as his little son in the face of
his destiny. His paternity, his power and his authority are only relative; he is himself quite as dependent
on other things as were his own father and grand-
parents, as will be his son and his grandchildren.
There is here an inevitable "alignment" that nothing
should allow us to forget. At the level of the created
being, the relationship of generation (the father-son
relationship) is only shared in a small way and represents only a distant and very imperfect analogy with
the divine paternity in itself and in relationship with
the rest of the world. In other words, God is the
Father of all, including human fathers. . . . He is at
the same time the Son, in Himself, and the Spirit of
interior Unity. It is to this knowledge of faith that
the child, when he in turn becomes an adult, should
attain.

Education in general and religious education in
particular should recognize these two basic realities
as being of the highest importance: first the child's
tendency to live in relationship with his father as an
absolute, and second the absolute transcendence of
the divine paternity. Experience shows that the traces
of the paternal image are very difficult to eliminate

from the religious dialogue, and that the tendency to "paternalize" God, or to fit Him into the human father relationship, is all too easy. Among many neurasthenics whose infantile conflicts are intense and still present in the unconscious, the spiritual life is sometimes greatly hindered through the transference, produced by such conflicts, in which God is conceived as a kind of "super-father."

It is therefore indispensable that the child should very early be able to discern, even if only dimly, the radical difference between his father and this *Someone* of whom people speak to him, and to whom he and all of us must speak on our knees. But it is also essential that the family environment be such that the inevitable emotional conflicts of the child be only in proportion to his stage of development and that they can be resolved.

In order to help the child through these difficult transitions the parental attitude is obviously of the greatest importance. It consists in a delicate balance between the necessary authority and the very relativity of this authority. The child needs to be protected, to be guided, to be corrected; but he also needs for his way to God not to be emotionally "blocked" by the paternal figure.

An inconsistent father, one more like his wife's oldest child (such cases may be obvious, or they may not be so obvious, but they are not so rare!) could not bring to his children the emotional security they need, nor the masculine authority they expect in one way or another following the trends of their sex. The child is "deceived" without knowing it by the paternal relationship as he experiences it, and is in danger of "grafting on to" God, about whom he has been told, the characteristics of the ideal father he lacks. Inversely there is also the danger that he may find no interest at all in this quest, that he may cling desperately to a kind of dependence upon his mother that will soon, moreover, become intolerable to him, and that he will never be able positively to become oriented toward the "Father who is in Heaven."

On the other hand, parents who are too absolutist in their educational attitude run the risk of provoking a different reaction. The confusion that can be caused in the profound emotional conditioning between the paternal authority and the divine authority can lead the child once he reaches adulthood to reject the idea of a God who is perfectly good when he perceives that his own father is not.

Or, again, if the religious sentiment is very strong in him, his passionate need for an ideal father runs the grave risk of being tainted by an antagonistic reaction to parental dictation and, without in the least suspecting it, the child will have the tendency to "requisition" God's support in his revolt. It is a curious fact worth noting that a large number of *avant-garde* thinkers who very easily confuse the divine with revolution in the temporal world have often received a strongly authoritarian education. Along the same line, certain "conservative" thinkers, who are not so very far from looking upon God as a kind of "All-Powerful Bogeyman," have often had tyrannical fathers who terrified them.

It is therefore absolutely necessary that the father be fully aware of the exact proportional worth of his own position. It is essential that he should know, and that he should make his children realize, that he is an authority but that he is not absolute. It is essential that he should make them understand very early that like themselves he, too, is capable of making mistakes; and that he, too, is engaged in the endless search for perfection. It is essential that he should know enough to apologize formally to his children, even when they are very young, for faults he has committed or mistakes he has unwittingly made. His children's confidence in him will be multiplied because of it: "You can tell Daddy anything because he is honest and he knows when he has been wrong." We wish we could hear this phrase more often on the lips of the little fellows in the catechism class! (The wish would be just as valid, indeed, if the reference were to the priest who composes the catechism, or the one who directs the youth club.) The way is thus opened for the search for that Father who does not make mistakes, and whose Love is so great that He has given His Son to the world in order to save it. It is opened also, to the greatest possible extent, to the mysterious action of this God now conceived as transcendent in the child's mind, in other words to grace.

Moreover, the religious attitude of the father himself must of necessity plan an important role; not only from the point of view of example—by no means a negligible factor—but from the point of view of this study: the emotional evolution of the child. The father not only makes the child understand that he himself is only relative, but he also helps him to understand his own need to refer to an absolute, his own trust in God's salvation. He tends through the child to give expression to the elementary reality that in the eyes of God they are almost at the same level; they are more *brothers* than father and son. This aspect of the problem is more easily understood by the boy because the process of identification, begun at the conclusion of the oedipus conflict, follows a little later on. There is a spontaneous dominant tendency in the masculine psychology, that we might call the pretension to understand everything by the light of reason, leading the man to reject or disregard whatever lies outside of this pretension. This tendency is opposed to the religious tendency, itself also spontaneous, to the extent sometimes of repressing it temporarily. Then the moment comes—let it be a serious illness, or some form of panic—and you will see the most rational of philosophers and scholars rushing to the faith healer or the quack polished up with pseudo-mysticism, or following in the steps of some escaped lunatic who brews up an incredible hash of mythological-theosophy around his own delirium of Christ-like reincarnation. . . .

As he grows up the man has to learn to balance these two tendencies so that, instead of canceling one another out, they may help to fertilize and develop one another. The rational tendency should help the mystical tendency to steer clear of the aberrations in which it is always liable to become involved; in the dynamic attitude of faith there is an important and continual work for the intelligence and the inescapable demands of reason. The mystical tendency should prevent the rational tendency from becoming so enlarged that it obscures the horizon; there is, in the relationship of the Faith between God and man, the necessity of a dialogue, wherein man, having arrived at a certain stage, keeps silence so that he may listen. But these tendencies, before they open out at the level of the consciousness and of the spirit, are deeply rooted in the emotional needs. It is therefore essential that the child should *feel* in an emotional manner a minimum of security around him. In the slow evolution of his confrontation and identification with his father, the boy should experience the need for acquiring this security for himself. Then the last reactions of opposition and of disentanglement from adolescence will permit him to develop his own spiritual life without infantile emotional dependence, and without anxiety in the face of his own autonomy. One of the most essential factors in religious education is very obviously that the parents should first themselves be authentically *religious* (and we need hardly add, for it goes without saying, that by this we do not mean bigots or legalists).

If the paternal figure—and all that is associated

with it in the educational domain—has a very great importance, the maternal figure is hardly less important although in a very different way. In the Christian environment it is in connection with the Blessed Virgin or with a certain conception of the Church that the problems arise. There would undoubtedly be plenty of scope to make a profound study of this point, but it would be a very long undertaking, involving observation and reflection. All we can do here is to mention certain aspects.

Here again the excessive or dominant persistence of infantile emotional reactions gravely increases the likelihood of falsifying or contaminating the objective perception of this mystery in all its transcendence. In this situation the subject has plenty of chances of grasping imperfectly what we could call the "theological dimension" of the Blessed Virgin; and of transforming her, unknown to himself, and in an implicit way, into a sort of protective spirit, the object of a cult that is more superstitious than anything else. This, unfortunately, happens all too often. It is quite enough to observe certain pilgrimages or visit certain shrines to be seized with a real uneasiness and disquiet. And too often one regrets that these great manifestations, sincere and undoubtedly capable of being turned to the best uses for the furtherance of the Faith, are not more enlightened by some solid teaching, and that they simply mark time in movements that become all the more emotional with the size of the crowd.

The person of the Blessed Virgin is the key to the Christian mystery just as she is the link between the Old and the New Testament. She is literally the Mother of God Incarnate. That is to say, she is the sole and unique door, the sole and unique means created by God to bring His real and saving presence into the world of men. But she is not merely that; that is only stating the essential. She is more than that—she is the only creature who is totally aware, without the slightest regression upon herself, of her condition as a creature, of her complete relativity in relationship with God, aware, that is, of her radical need of God which is the need of all humanity. But she has not, strictly, anything divine or semi-divine in herself; she is the transparent habitation of God.

We are very far here from the concept of an emotional, sensibly protective maternity that is embodied in far too many texts and habitual formulae. The danger of the vocabulary is very clearly manifested here: in order to express the inexpressible we only have at our disposal symbols that too easily fail or deceive. Just as God is called Father, so the Blessed Virgin will be called Mother. But here, too, this maternity has nothing to do with an emotional intra-family relationship: it is a theological maternity, mystical in the real sense of this word, and universal.

We think that a very great effort is called for to clear up this point in the religious education of children. In this matter, too, the exact attitude of the parents in their own religious practice is of primordial importance for the reasons just given. But what will be said in the course of instruction has a considerable importance, too; at each moment, and progressively, we must help the child to break away from a devotional attitude that could involve him in a retarded and dominant emotionalism. Finally—and this goes for all the demands of religious education—it is necessary for mothers to start very early to teach their children gradually to do without them as much as they can, so that when they reach the stage of adulthood they may be in a position to do so fully. Thus as autonomous adults they will discover in its mystical purity the need to be born again into the world of the Risen Christ given to man by God through the transcendental motherhood of Mary.

The word "Church" is equally, it would seem, the

subject of various ambiguous interpretations. It, too, is classified as a feminine word and very often joined to the word "Mother" in current religious parlance. "Our Holy Mother the Church" is a phrase in point. But in this matter, too, for a true conception of the mystery of the Church it is necessary to leave behind completely any primitive emotional attitudes. The individual mind can make only an approach to a perception of this mystery; but it is essential that such an approach be made, and that it should tend more and more to a conception that in clarity, realism and fullness corresponds most closely to its transcendence. Emotional retardations have the curious but logical effect of limiting the concept of the Church to its human, temporal and, let us say, administrative aspects. It is no longer the "home" of the human race in its general historical and spatial context, in its true relation with God, the Creator and Redeemer. It is a collection of ecclesiastical and semi-ecclesiastical organizations, with rites, customs and rules. For anyone who is not a part of its "administrative groups" such an organization becomes a superior and anonymous entity upon which he is dependent and in which he shares as someone ruled but not as a living member. It is by no means paradoxical to state that this devaluation of the Church is very widespread in the world at large; it is enough to note the need for a review of the situation from what is coming to light in current research upon the laity's concept of its theological function.

In the face of an administration on a world-wide scale, strongly organized and conceived of as "Our Mother," a reaction of childish dependence may become so strong that the mystical aspect—which in the long run takes precedence over and keeps the other aspect in existence—is hardly perceived or else is passed over in silence. The consequences may be contradictory. Where the reaction is one of direct

childish or infantile dependence the effect will be a
tendency to confuse the values and to give an absolute significance to completely secondary details.
Obedience will be passive, turning chiefly upon such
details, instead of a personal, free and voluntary adherence to what makes up the essence of the mystery
of the Church. Or, on the other hand, the reaction
is one of dependence but of an antagonistic nature;
there will be the tendency to criticize—always on the
matter of these details—and to reject an entity of
which only the smallest aspects and inevitable weaknesses have been perceived, without any realization
of the fact that it is a mystical community. In other
words, emotional infantilism tends to rob the visible
Church to which we are subject of its real mystical
significance, or else to rob the mystical Church, to
which we adhere, of the visible and organized expression that is absolutely indispensable to it. Thus, by
its tendency to dissociate the essential unity of these
two aspects, emotional infantilism gravely affects the
subjective conception of the Church.

There are many instances of these two regressive
attitudes. When an unimportant prelate, but one who
lives in Rome, publishes in some bulletin or other in
Italian a set of absolutely personal opinions on some
subject of which he knows very little (this has happened several times and seems to be inevitable),
someone will be bound immediately to accept such
an utterance as Gospel truth, and *will not be able* to
realize that the whole thing has nothing to do with
the magistery of the Church. Or again someone else,
highly intelligent and genuinely religious, will be
equally *unable* to stop himself from constantly criti-
cizing the Holy Church, because of his unconscious
and unrecognizable need to extricate himself from the
heritage of a neurotic mother who has ruined his life.

Here again, in order for the child to be able to attain progressively to a correct and synthesized con-

ception of the Church, it is important at least that his education shall not impede him.

To be successful in teaching others, parents and educators should first of all cultivate this correct conception in themselves, and by their habitual behavior should promote those reactions that correspond to it. Parents for whom the parish priest represents a kind of "Holy-God-policeman-dictator" or for whom, at the other extreme, he is always a narrow-minded old fogy whom, they are obliged to support, are obviously ill-fitted to surround their children with a basically necessary atmosphere of loyal adherence to the mystery of the Church. As we are on the subject, we might add that a dictatorial and cantankerous parish priest runs the strong danger of doing little to aid the children in his school and parish to discover the mystery of the priesthood through him.

In the family environment, too, the requirements are the same as for the problem of devotion to the Blessed Virgin. The mother must do all she can to make it easy for the children to pass toward adult autonomy in relationship with her. They cannot be true "children of the Church" save to the extent that they no longer feel the emotional need to be the children of a woman.

In the preceding chapters we have many times referred to the idea of frustration. The child, in order to follow the normal course of his emotional evolution, must be able to "renounce" [1] one way of life in order to accede to another more autonomous and therefore more satisfying, although more difficult and more demanding. If all were to go well—if, in other words, the world were not under the sign of sin—

---

[1] This term is also analogous. Analogy of movement: to leave one thing for something else. But it is quite obvious that this cannot yet be a conscious step in the moral or spiritual order.

these successive transitions would be achieved in the progressive and complete expansion of a dynamism which was continuously more giving and communicating and free. But the reality is different. We have seen many times that emotional evolution is marked by a certain inevitable lag between the rate of the child's emotional maturity and the demands of his growth and development. The "sentiment" of frustration, in varying degrees with different children, is therefore inevitable. It corresponds directly to the impression of failure or of non-achievement, which is the same thing. The progress through the different stages is in certain measure painful, because it involves a kind of uprooting, as if the child, still clinging to the unfulfilled emotional need that dominates his life at that moment, is torn by the forward step and the fundamental urge to discover wider fields.

But this clinical phenomenon, one of central importance from the viewpoint of modern psychology, carries a singular and striking parallel to the Christian vision of the world and of its destiny from the fact that here, too, an absolutely central idea is the one of failure overcome or survived and of suffering that redeems. "Lord, who by Thy death hast renewed the world," is found in the liturgical text of the Mass; herein resides the key to all Christian doctrine; God has come to dwell personally in our suffering and in our supreme failure of death in order to transform these into victory. In other words, by the light of His Word and His actions we understand that temporal life is itself only an unfulfilled stage. In the same way that taking nourishment by sucking is only transitory, the temporal way of life is only a passing step in the evolution toward access to the absolute life—eternal life—destined for us by Divine Love. It is always necessary for something to die in order that life may triumph more profoundly. In this perspective death appears as the supreme birth and the supreme expansion. In the same way suffering appears as the palpable proof of a movement toward completion and fulfillment.

In this supernatural vision of the human drama man should not be fettered by an emotional resistance or blockage from making his own and putting to the fullest use the frustrations of life. On the other hand, the basic depths or origins of his emotional life should not be so oppressed by hardships that, in his instinctive reaction to them, man is unable to pass freely through the various stages of his development. From birth to adolescence it is important that he should not suffer *too much* through the inevitable frustrations involved in his evolution.

Here is where the emotional atmosphere in which the child grows up assumes a paramount importance in his subsequent religious evolution. In the first years, it is even more essential than moral teaching that the child should acquire the habit of living, in other words, not just drifting through a passing collection of tastes and needs. It is essential for him to be able to emerge from, and in a certain sense to forget, a way of life that is content with sensory satisfaction. To achieve this he must first of all have tested it sufficiently and at the same time come progressively to realize its inadequacy and its transience. Education does not consist in letting the child do everything he wishes; nor does it mean plunging him at once into an atmosphere of hardship and intensive restraint that may bring out the worst in him. A child should be happy but he should not become fixed, as it were, on a current state of happiness. The child who is tyrannized and the spoiled child will both have plenty of difficulty later on in trying to integrate the various frustrations of life and in accepting the true Christian mystery of death. It is through the emotional dynamism first of all and not through ideas or principles of behavior that the psychological foundations are prepared for the building of a healthy religious attitude in the very young child. This smile or that just reproof, gentle but firm, do more sometimes in this sense than the recitation of prayers: it is very important that these latter should correspond, as far as the child is concerned, with life as he knows it.

Sexual Education

Finally, we must touch upon the delicate question of sexual education. Experience shows what an important part the problems of the sexual life play in the formation of a religious attitude, and draws attention to the grave mistakes still being made in this matter, or to the gaps that still exist.

The paradox of sexuality consists in the fact that it is one of the most intense of the psycho-emotional powers, but that in the spiritual synthesis of the personality it is of only secondary importance. It is only a register of the manifestations of the personality, but this register has particularly important reverberations. . . . If sexual problems are not well cleared up and put into their proper place, they seriously risk becoming a constraint and sometimes even an obstacle to a genuine religious attitude.

The scope of sexual education should be examined in order to see precisely what it involves. Briefly the point is that the subject, having arrived at puberty, should have control of his sexual power and be able to orient it in accordance with his free choice. Theoretically speaking, the young man or the young woman should be able, in accordance with the personal and free orientation of their lives, to take the positive preliminary steps in continence for the conjugal situation which they desire, or to undertake and commit themselves to the way of perpetual continence for reasons of a higher order. In other words, and ideally speaking always, a subject on the threshold of adulthood should be able to live chastely if he wishes to, and either to exercise his sexual power or to consecrate it in transcending it.

But this ideal development can only be conceived in a religious view of things and on condition that a theological meaning is given to the reality of sex. Since sexuality is the power of relational and procreative love, it is in the rational, created, human being an analogous participation, very remote but direct, in the mystery of God Himself. "And God created man to his own image; to the image of God he created them. Male and female he created them" (Genesis 1:27). From this standpoint the emotional and physical joy of sexual fulfillment cannot be conceived at its true worth except in the significance of both personal love and the power of generation that it carries in God's plan. Apart from this significance it becomes literally monstrous, like some vital disorder or some degrading travesty. In Christian logic, of course, sexual fulfillment can only be conceived of as just and positively good when it involves the conjugal relation of two people permanently united.

Furthermore, this sexual fulfillment ought to be conceived as something that has every reason and right to be good and desirable. The young subject should have a clear, free, orderly and objectively exact conception of all that it means. In other words, he should have all the elements of emotional maturity and theoretical knowledge that will enable him to make, actually and existentially, this necessary synthesis.

What is one to think, then, of a so-called Christian education that leaves the child, the adolescent and finally the young man in ignorance and incomprehension of what takes place in him and of the meaning, human and spiritual, of his growth? Or which through an unhealthy shame allows him to pick up incoherent information for himself from the most dubious sources? Or when any illusion to this immense problem is made in veiled, confused and vague terms and then only under the aspect of mortal sin? Or which allows the young people to understand—not by explicit teaching, to be sure, but by the absence of any definite statement—that this sin is indeed the only sin, the most important and the most serious, an idea that is theologically false if reference be made, among others, to St. Thomas? It seems to us that we should think of such "education" as neither human nor Christian, that is all. Yet despite the progress made by modern psychology, despite the frequent reminders of the hierarchy of the Church, is this scandalous method of miseducation still so very rare? Even more perhaps than in other domains of life, dread and ignorance are anti-educational forces in the matter of sexuality. The spiritual and psychological danger is grave, and it cannot be too often repeated that, paradoxically and all too frequently, such ignorance ends in a veritable pansexualism. The subject thus unarmed is in danger of living now in a hypertrophic and quasi-obsessional preoccupation with his sexuality that prevents him from approaching a true spiritual synthesis.

Once again, in this as in the previous problems, the emotional environment in which the child grows up has quite as much importance as anything he is told. Or, to put it in a different way, whatever he is told will not be really effective and fruitful unless it comes to him in a certain environment and atmosphere.

The point is that in the course of the first emotional stages of his life the child should enter into an instinctive and positive acceptance of his own sex; that he should not be afraid of it; and that he should not have any impression of being either overvalued or undervalued because of it. One of the first conditions for this evolution being achieved correctly is again the real harmony of the parental couple. But harmony should also be fostered and encouraged in the continuous relationships of the child with each of his parents and with other children.

With regard to what is told to him, it is very clear from the start that it must be nothing but the truth —as much of it as he asks for and is capable of receiving and understanding in a completely simple and natural order of things. If "Santa Claus" and the "stork" are to be proscribed on the grounds of mental health so much the more should they be excluded on the grounds of Christian education.

We cannot set forth here all the details of this education. Our thesis is confined to drawing the attention of readers not only to its importance but to its links with all the rest of the work of education. Parents and educators who wish to be faithful to the demands of their role have every good reason to keep themselves informed methodically through the medium of the excellent publications that have appeared in recent years on these different problems, excluding, of course, such as are materialist in their outlook or are written from a slanted viewpoint.

VIII
God
the
Creator

Not so long ago in one of the secondary colleges of a large provincial town the priest giving a retreat made a stupefying discovery. Before he started he outlined a scheme he had for sermons to be given to the older pupils, intending to develop some of the main biblical themes and to give a commentary on certain passages in Holy Scripture. The response to his suggestion shocked him: "The Bible? . . . But they have not been taught anything about the Bible since elementary school. They will not understand you. . . ."

This means that in this school (and it is one of the best), and doubtless in a great many others, the boys had reached the college level with a religious stock of knowledge consisting solely of the "Bible history" of their early childhood. To be sure year after year they had been given instruction in the form of "Christian Doctrine" as elaborated by the works of pious and serious writers; morality and/or ethics had been given in some detail and dogmas had been defined. But all this had been resting on memories becoming more and more hazy of something which these young men were incapable, in fact, of distinguishing from pure legend. After the age of ten, these boys had no further methodical and consistent contact with the Word of God as written in the history of man. They had been given, instead, an abstract elaboration cut off from its roots. Consequently when they attained the age of seventeen or eighteen, the age when the spirit of criticism begins to develop acutely and especially against the background of the scientific outlook so widespread today, they had no tool of any value with which they could constructively build up their adult religious attitude.

Certainly the considerable effort of the catechetical revival is tending to thrust back into the past such methods of dealing with religious education. But there is every advantage in helping to intensify this effort by dwelling on the heavy handicap that burdens the progress of children formed by such methods. Whatever vague notions they have retained of Noah, of Abraham and of Moses cannot be very far removed from what might be called "old wives' tales." Since they are no longer thrilled in the same way by the "marvels" that held them spellbound in their childhood, and since no one has taken text in hand to show them the theological and perfectly real and substantial dimension of Sacred Scripture, the vital center of their Faith is threatened. Will they all be capable of the immense effort necessary to shake off completely the retarded puerilities that at this age have become intolerably irritating to some of them? Will they all be able to give full glory and profound significance to names they have heard only in the distant past? Can the very names of "Jesus" and "Mary" be brusquely divorced from the childhood spell they once cast but which—properly at this age— seems heartbreakingly remote and insipid?

We have barely touched upon the fact that since the elementary grades they had been taught nothing further about the Bible. How can this void be filled? We recall how personally we had to wait until the age of thirty, when we commenced our theological studies in preparation for the priesthood, before we

knew and could place Ezechiel and the author of the
Canticles, and that was after long years at the university. But what of our fellow students who turned
to different professions—how much did they retain
of the early instruction they received? In questioning
an average student one is frequently overwhelmed by
his ignorance of Holy Scripture. Recently one of
them told us that he knew of the New Testament
just this much: that it contained the Gospel—without
any further details—and the Epistles; but as to who
the authors of these were, or what they were all
about. . . . And here we are speaking of a good student, one remaining loyal to the practice of his religion—the future "average practicing Catholic"!

It is difficult to restrain an outburst of indignation
when one encounters this neglect of the Word of God.
It is a miracle that young men still keep what is
called "the Faith" when nothing is done to help them
to discover and to follow the flow and progressive
development of the message of God in its historical
and absolutely real context.

Judeo-Christian Revelation

Now the Judeo-Christian Revelation is, in itself,
but the history of an education. In one sense it is
also the history of an education type; and through
modern psychology we are able to understand it better and to grasp its supreme realism.

During the course of two thousand years the people
chosen by God for His purpose of precipitating Himself personally into human history were being prepared attentively, progressively and with infinite respect for their liberty. God, if we may dare so to
express it, warned but did not constrain His people,
and He did not prevent them from committing inevitable blunders. But at each stage He consoled,
He explained, He encouraged. In the course of suc-

cessive and more or less dramatic experiences He aided His people to draw lessons from their own history as they had lived it; His Prophets helped the faithful core to discover vistas ever vaster and more and more complex and developed. He brought His people to the stage of self-knowledge, and perhaps the most arresting aspect of Holy Scripture to be noted is this evolution of religious thought from chaos and myth and from which the Jewish people alone were able to emerge.

The fact is unique in the religious history of the human race. For the point of departure of the Judeo-Christian religion is the same as that of all the other peoples in the ancient East. Abraham was a Chaldean. That is to say, the religious conceptions amid which this *historical* person lived before his departure for the desert were a confused mixture of mythology, animism and magic. The cultural mentality of these people, although very complex from the technical point of view, for instance, was still almost completely primitive in respect of thought. In two thousand years of history the descendants of Abraham, first of all nomadic, then settled, pass from naïve and primitive "magic" to the highest philosophical development achieved by the human spirit—the idea of the Trinity, the knowledge of God, One in Three, in other words, the dim and mysterious perception of living Revelation and of absolute Love.

For this the continual educative Presence of God was needed, introducing Itself in the most definite and real way into the very depths of the mentality of the men to whom He spoke. The infinitely perfect Educator, God, carried His people through the various stages of their development, complying, if one might put it thus, with their own language and with the tenor of their ways, urging "from within" as well as by means of His spokesmen this transcendent evolution of thought and of the religious sense.

Why do not educators studiously and methodically draw inspiration from the "instructive procedures" of God Himself? Why does not religious education in our times follow step by step this education of the chosen people as historically achieved in other times? We are a long way, unfortunately, from the methods of St. Augustine or St. Cyril of Jerusalem. . . . We may well ask in some astonishment why religious education is not centered around the study of Holy Scripture, enlightened by the interpretation and the endless labor of the Church. The biblical revival finally launched during recent years seems at least to be starting some response to this primordial demand.

Primitive Peoples and Child Psychology

There is a good deal of talk today of primitive peoples, of childlike peoples, and of the growth of civilizations. It is quite true to say that those who employ such terms are not speaking altogether allegorically. There is a certain analogy, a genuine resemblance, between the mentality of a primitive civilization and the early stages of the child's psychology. That, however, does not mean that they are the same thing, that primitive tribes react at all points like children, or that their perception of the world is the same. But it is undeniable, and indeed a recognized fact, that there are to be found in the mentality of primitive peoples certain reactions of the infantile type. The personification of natural forces, such as storms, and crediting them with souls and deliberate intentions—which is at the root of all mythologies—correspond to the first spontaneous methods of acquiring knowledge tried by the child. Imagining that thought or desire has some direct power over things and events—an illusion underlying all magic conceptions and superstitions—characterizes the spontaneous reactions of the child before the development of his rational potentialities. The collective childhood of civilizations shares, though in a different way, in the prelogical or "magic" mentality that is characteristic of the childhood of each individual member of the human race.

Now the Jewish people at the beginning of their history, namely, at the time when Abraham and his tribe broke away from the rest of the Chaldeans, were still a primitive people, a civilization in a state of infancy. Their later history, the very substance of the Bible, is nothing other than the progressive growth toward an adult mentality regarding the relations of man with God. This achievement—once again unique in history—is impressive by reason of its coherence, its unity and its transcendence. Without forcing the comparison to an extreme degree, one can observe it in the same way one would the psychological evolution of a human being, and recognize in it—always in an analogous way—the actual stages of growth. An examination of the history of the chosen people from this standpoint could be a source of infinite profit if methodically aligned with a more objective plan of religious education—a plan concerned not only with the living Revelation of the Word of God but also with the concrete reality of the human psychology destined to receive it.

The patriarchal period corresponds to what might be called the early childhood of the chosen people. They were separated from their native environment; under the leadership of Abraham they embarked upon a strange and wandering isolation. Right from the start they were distinguished by concern for this separateness, or more precisely for the unique character and mission thereof. They were to do all they could to understand it, at the same time keeping up contact with neighboring tribes and nations as if to increase their self-knowledge by opposition. The same conflicts were to serve them for consolidating and protecting their individuality, a little like the small child in relation with the people around him. The chosen people were like the rest of men, in the midst of them and sharing the same nature and the same origin as their neighbors, but they were the only ones to "be themselves" if we may risk such an expression. What made them specifically themselves was the dialogue with the true, mysterious and transcendent Divinity.

But they were still permeated by the superstitious mentality of those primitive times. The story of Genesis is, from this point of view, absolutely remarkable in its ambivalence: it is marked by considerable traces of the "myth" mentality and of superstition, yet at the same time one finds therein an already pre-eminent development of religious thought boldly detaching itself from this mentality in indisputable and historical reality. In fact, a number of the elements of the biblical story are to be found in ancient Babylonian documents. The verbal and symbolical material of the latter is obviously colored—it could not be otherwise—by the content of pagan traditions, yet at the same time everything is changing. What before had no mission to instruct now had something to say. What before were only myths expressing human anguish or human hopes now became coherent, historic and explanatory of the essential discovery: God is ONE, living, absolutely transcendent, the Creator. He revealed Himself sufficiently for them to recognize His existence and to conduct His dialogue with them. But He revealed Himself by using the very framework of primitive thought and even its imagery. He did not set out a highly elaborate metaphysic, but already, within this existing framework with its still magic hue, He gave an inkling of what was to come. We have only to recall that the covenant He made with Noah was signalized by the symbol of a rainbow which allowed for animistic beliefs; we have only to follow the development and purification of the idea of the covenant from this point up to the texts of the Canticle of Canticles, for example, and then up to the personality of Christ as it appears at the discourse during the Last Supper according to St. John, chapters 15, 16, and 17.

It was by using the magic beliefs of a people in the childhood of their civilization that God helped them progressively to outgrow them; from a primitive predilection for direct action of the will or for rites following the rhythms of nature they were slowly to pass to the idea of a supreme, voluntary, unforeseeable and significant action of God upon the world, that is to say, to the idea of a miracle. The traces of magic were to persist for long enough: the constant recourse of the Patriarchs of "lots," for instance, has not the same meaning as the choosing of the replacement for Judas that takes place in the Acts of the Apostles: it is nothing more here than a working procedure, whereas among the Patriarchs it was still literally an occult practice. Moreover, animism was to linger for a long time: the Jews were to attribute active personalities to the stars in accordance with the traditions of the Babylonians; and centuries and all the work of the Prophets were needed in order to bring forth the knowledge of the angelic world.

This comparison of the chosen people with a human personality and its growth is suggested to us in the Sacred Scripture itself. The Prophet Ezechiel's admirable chapter 16 is entirely built upon this suggestion: "Thus saith the Lord God to Jerusalem: Thy root and thy nativity is of the land of Canaan. Thy father was an Amorite and thy mother a Cethite." . . . Then there is the history, symbolically recounted, of the Jewish nation: its education by Jehovah, its dramas, its infidelities, its punishment, its return and the promise of union re-established, stronger and deeper, thanks to its trials.

From the childhood of the patriarchal period the Jewish people were led into the Egyptian captivity. This community of people, still very primitive in culture and yet completely inspired by an authentic religious quest, were now to be confronted by a civilization that was very adult on the human plane. It was to pick up from it elements of thought and of "wisdom" that were never to disappear from its traditions and to detach them from their limited significance in order to relate them to the Word of the One and Living God. But in Egypt it was also to meet with captivity, downfall and the triumphant challenge of a new uprooting. From Joseph to Moses the people, first happy then severely tried, emerged through knowledge and suffering from their primitive and childlike mentality. They were to learn more of their mission and of the demands it involved; they were once more ready to "cut the cord," stifling as it was in this pagan and sterile civilization with its spectacular and grandiose prosperity. Aware of its own personality, they were to oppose this alien culture, by force, if necessary, and to leave Egypt, just as the adolescent opposes his family environment and seeks to break out from a framework that has become inadequate.

So once again the tribe of Abraham was launched upon the great adventure. Alone. In the desert. For almost seven centuries the people were to wrestle with their special destiny in continual alternation between the longing for a temporal and political establishment so nearly realized under Solomon, and dreary dissatisfaction with fulfillments that crumbled away as if through some inner corruption.

In this anxiety of doubt, in this dramatic confrontation with their own autonomy and the vast and hostile world surrounding them, the Jewish people reacted like the adolescent struggling with the sudden advent of his powers: they were to barricade themselves around with numerous "life lines" of precepts, rites and prescribed rules. This was the legalistic period, and this outlook was to last a very long time in Jewish history, indeed up to the day of Christ, and was even to sink into the hateful caricature of Pharisaism.

The danger was subtle and serious: the legal precepts which were but a means to illustrate in a certain standard way a stage of development in the intercourse with God were in danger of being taken for absolute values and thereby of forming an obstacle to the continuing intercourse itself. When this happens things are limited to a mutual confrontation between the legal precepts and the individual in what amounts to an extreme narcissistic quest for some reassuring satisfaction. This, of course, is nothing more nor less than the revival of the spirit of original sin. Since in any vital aspect or condition such immobilization can only mean relapse and regression, there is danger of returning to a certain "magic," a primitive and superstitious concept of these rites and precepts. This is again an evidence of the human desire and will to act directly and not to await God in His quest for communion with man. Finally there is the danger of losing a clear perception of the inherent transitoriness and relative character of these temporal satisfactions—individual or collective—a perception that these same precepts and rites are intended to promote.

It is the very situation of the adolescent and the young man. It is indeed the very situation of every man right up to the time of his death that he may allow himself to be lured by this moral narcissism and the longing for a temporal realization of his desires that would be absolute.

But the Kingdom of God triumphed beyond the

prison of passing time. And God, by all the means proportionate to the current actual mentality of His chosen people, was to continue His teaching, helping His faithful community to emerge from the legalistic rut and to see progressively the transcendent horizons which were theirs. He was to awaken the demands and the awareness of hope, He was to speak, using human language that was severe, tender or even appealing, addressing Himself to all that was living and unselfish in the human heart. This is the tenor of thought of the Prophets who unremittingly pointed out the error of legalism, appealed to the spirit and explained the meaning of trials. Why is not the religious teaching of adolescents and young people centered around this primordial spiritual treasure, and based on a methodical and profound study of Jeremia, of Isaia and of Ezechiel?

For, like the Jewish people in the monarchical period of their history, the adolescent and the young man come up against failure and suffer because they do not understand. And, like the adolescent deceived in his idealistic hopes, the Jewish people saw themselves conquered, stunned, sorrowful in the anguish and grief of their deportation to Babylon between the years 587 and 538 before our Christian era.

In these somber years, as during the following centuries, in the midst of struggles, invasions, before their powerlessness to build the temporal and religious kingdom they knew to have been promised them, the faithful core of the chosen people reflected upon and sought to understand the meaning of this suffering. Such is the overwhelming nostalgia expressed in Psalm 136: "Upon the rivers of Babylon, there we sat and wept . . ." Such is the song of faith and hope triumphant on the threshold of despair in Psalm 129: "Out of the depths I have cried to thee, O Lord: Lord, hear my voice. . . ." Such is the long religious meditation of the historical books. By

what misunderstanding, by what infidelities, had
the chosen people of God arrived at such an ebb of
misery, at such tragic failure? What was the meaning, more profound and more mysterious even than
is supposed, of this perilous and indeed disastrous
period in their history? What, above all, was the
ultimate meaning of unmerited suffering such as
Job's—suffering that was not a chastisement since
Job had observed the Law, but which was indeed a
mystery? Then, little by little, the idea dawned that
death is not the end of all but is, on the contrary,
the solution to the problem. There is another life
than the one lived in time—this affirmation is not
made clear in Holy Scripture until the time of the
Maccabees at the end of the second century before
Christ. The precise prophecy of the Messiah, suffering, triumphant, and redeeming because He sacrifices
His life is given in Isaia.

Now Christ could come. The faithful core of the
people—those who had not been swamped by riches
or power, or by surrender to idols, or by the routine
of the legalistic traditions—was ready to attain to
adulthood in religious life and knowledge. Without
yet being clearly aware of it, these faithful children
of God had virtually transcended the anxieties and
the frightening doubts of adolescence; they were dy-
namically prepared; nothing held or imprisoned them
in their past; they were able to continue on the
road God was leading them and to achieve the stag-
gering revolution of the Christian Church. The
certainty of the Resurrection, the light of Easter
finally revealed, the hope of the Kingdom of God
which is stronger than the fears and anxieties of the
temporal kingdom—such are the characteristics of
the apostolic and Christian age, of the adulthood of
religious evolution. And without any doubt it was
"presided over" by one who was always completely
open and ready to receive the living Mystery, com-

pletely free in her acquiescence to Absolute Love, one who was by unique privilege and as a proof of the instructive patience of God, the perfect adult and the creature who was totally fulfilled. It was the Blessed Virgin who presided at Pentecost, that historic moment when all become clear, when everything assumed its proper place and was set going, that moment when the Hebrew boundaries burst apart to give birth to the Church of Christ.

For a human being, the drama of his own destiny is comparable at all points to this drama of the Jewish community which through the course of the centuries learned laboriously to transcend the illusions of time. He, too, must learn, in the course of his childhood and of his youth, the joy of life. He, too, must learn that this joy has real value only because life is eternal and his life in time is only a stage, that death is nothing but the last threshold to be crossed. How better could he learn all this than by following, age after age, the history of the people of God? How could educators and parents help him better than by the inspiration of God's own "educational method"? Briefly, this is but a matter of living up to the requirements of a love that is real.

Some Additional Reflections

There is a good deal of discussion about the "education of the will," but, as the subject is currently understood, if one adheres to the concepts of classical psychology which draws a distinction between the different "faculties," most of the time it will be found that we are not dealing with the will in the sense in which it is understood by, for example, St. Thomas Aquinas. During the course of the past few centuries indeed there has been a "writing down" of the meaning of the word, and when one speaks of "training the will" one is referring to a certain very superficial, psycho-physiological force of instantaneous action and not the vital, autonomous and unique dynamism of the spirit that St. Thomas identifies with Love. When a child is described as "lacking in will" it is commonly meant that he carries out painfully and reluctantly a decision he himself has not made and which has been imposed on him without attention being paid to what might help him to will it personally and happily.

Rarely, on the other hand, is there much talk about the "education of the intelligence," or of the "faculty of knowing." From this point of view the development of the exact sciences and technology, the ever-increasing and more complex requirements demanded by the procuring of diplomas and other academic or technical qualifications that have become essential for "getting on in life," present some serious dangers. Yet these dangers could be averted if educationists thought about how to provide against them without thereby adversely affecting the demands of modern education.

The danger of overwork and of psycho-nervous unbalance has already been vigorously stressed by specialists, and we shall not dwell upon this aspect here. But by a strange paradox education that is dominated by the demands of an objective and scientific outlook often runs the risk of resulting in a lack of objectivity. From this there can develop in a young person a real complex of living caused by a kind of "narcissism of the intelligence" of a character that can be either anxious or complacent according to the different types of subjects and their emotional situations. This complex amounts to a dividing up of reality into separate parts and even, in a way, of mutilating it through seeing only the quantitative or utilitarian aspect of the world even on the part of those engaged in the most advanced physico-chemical investigations. Almost imperceptibly the subjects of this complex come to the point that they will neither see nor acknowledge anything in the universe that they cannot control or submit to their interests. Imperceptibly they come to the point of *refusing to see* whatever cannot be confined within the boudaries of this so-called scientific or technical investigation, and consequently of refusing to acknowledge the profound significance of the universe and, in the proper sense of the word, its mystery. Imperceptibly in this uncomprehending outlook, they also come to the point of confusing human reality with everything else in their field of research, that is to say, they come to the point of treating man himself as an object of exclusively scientific interest. Man seen as a unit only is the result of the exaggerated outlook of physiology or mathematical biology; man viewed in a collective aspect only is the error of certain schools of sociology.

There is potential here for considerable regression, the results of which we can see at once for ourselves as much in Marxism as in certain sociological patterns characterized by an exaggerated individualism. The idol of scientific technology accepts impartially the sacrifice of the masses or the sacrifice of the individual. . . .

In either manifestation of this erroneous thinking, everything is done as though in the careful effort to develop in the child a detached mentality suited to the pursuit of the exact sciences, one has forgotten to help him to develop his existential relations with the world and to deal with other of his questions— not scientific but much vaster in scope. And in this world of complex existential relations one must face the fact of the powerlessness of truth to make itself known. If asked for a definition of truth, how many modern men with this outlook would be capable of replying that it consists in a harmony between thought and action, and this despite the fact that in the technical and scientific domain they know very well that truth consists in their acknowledging and conforming with the overwhelming existent reality of the object of their research?

Now in real life as we live it in actual practice— which is the domain of morality—the truth is also a reality. A person is *true*—and not merely sincere, which is something of secondary importance—to the extent that he recognizes existence outside himself and accepts the system of relations in which he stands thereto. The very basis of honesty of intellect consists in a sublimation of the power of knowledge.

As far as philosophical thought is concerned, what is needed is a return to the Thomist concept of man as a being whose existence has the twofold aspect of relation to self and relation to other than self, both aspects forming one real unity, and the harmonizing of this concept with modern modes of expression.

With his wonderful command of language, Claudel, in certain passages of his work, breaks out into one of his typically luminous expressions and writes "co-born." [1] that is, born with. To know [1] is to arrive at existence in relation to the other person whoever he may be. The discovery of a person other than myself and the relation between us increases me both in contrast with the other and in a communion of recip-rocal relations. We do not then exist, in the limited sense of this term, we co-exist." And the more we recognize the other from this point of view the more we exist—and the more we are *true*.

And this other is, in addition to being the other whom I see, this earth on which I walk, this dog that barks at me on my way, this friend "with whom I am born" time and again in the course of our com-mon pilgrimage, this woman "with whom I am born" each day again in the sacrament of love, God Him-self "with whom I am born" each day again to eternal life.

How important, from the educational point of view, is this primordial conception! We cannot love—that is to say, we cannot live and deepen our spiritual lives in the religious sense of the word—unless we have learned very early, emotionally and intellectu-ally, to be "born with" the other in this call to rela-tionship. It is not a matter of formulation of abstract and rationalist "principles," more or less Cartesian in character, but much more a matter of actual edu-cation and of the progressive expansion of the vital faculty of knowing within a true morality. Each created being, human or animal, however different the standards of intrinsic value may be, is an object of

---

[1] The point of our author's remarks in this and the next two paragraphs is not so effective in translation as in the original French, as the device he is using to drive home his argument is a pun upon the word *co-naître*, "co-born," and *connaître*," to know."—*Translator's Note.*

respect. To respect means *to look to* of one's own volition—which is already love—to recognize the object of one's gaze as existent and as *other*. To know is already to love; to love is already to know.

Value of Temporal Life

If the driving force of Christianity tends toward an ideal, Christianity for all that is not an idealism. By this I mean that it does not condemn the value of the temporal state as illusory and therefore as positively bad. In Christian eyes, in other words, this temporal life, in its most mundane and down-to-earth reality, is worth living. Not that it possesses an absolute and final value, but because human nature as it exists—even though "damaged"—is an incomplete work of value and because it was this condition that God assumed in order to make us whole by His death and Resurrection.

In a truly Christian religious education parents and teachers should know how to develop—in its proper place and in the right perspective—the taste for temporal life and its values. Modern psychology shows us that the child can arrive at school age with sufficient emotional elasticity and potential only if he has been *suitably* (neither too much nor too little) satisfied in his earlier needs. The adult can come freely to eternal life only if he has known the joy of temporal life in its true dimension—at once worthwhile and yet inadequate. If he has not known this, he cannot support his condition and he will, by a seeming paradox, pass through the successive stages of his development seeking, unknown to himself, an unrealizable absolute that will prevent him taking roots in the reality in which he exists and that hides from him the immediate demands of his situation. I have in mind now a parachutist who led an impressively heroic existence during the war years and yet, when peace returned, was incapable of adapting himself to the much less spectacular—but how much richer and more genuine!—demands of his family and social life. This is Baudelaire's *Albatross:* "Its giant wings hindered it from walking. . . ." But the prosaic *terra firma* has its own immediate interest for the very simple reason that it is our own soil and that we live on it! There is a wise old saying to the effect that "he who wishes to turn into an angel plays the fool." The important thing for us to do is to *play the man,* that fleshly condition that is good in itself. God saw that it was good—although fallen, deposed, ravaged—and yet in the final analysis it was deemed by and with and in the Risen Christ.

The Christian who has arrived at adulthood must engage in the tremendous battle of daily life and have *at the same time* the will to achieve perfection in all things and the certain knowledge that such perfection can be fully realized only in the next world. Nevertheless, unless he is fully determined to achieve this perfection in this world, the next world is no more to him than an intellectual concept. The Kingdom of Heaven is already among us. As St. Augustine says: "When you do something, do it as if the fate of the world depended upon it and *at the same time* as if you were to die at that moment and that it would not matter."

Religious Education and Balanced Living

A religious education that is really consistent with the receptive potentialities of the child and with the Word of God ought to be an essential factor in developing psychological balance. And not only by the simple method of natural development. Such education consists in fact—and this should never be forgotten—in encouraging the child to enter into a personal and living relationship with Someone. This

Someone, in the dialogue which He seeks in the very heart of man, has His word to say. In the mystery of His action, of His love, of His solicitude, He has as unreservedly committed Himself as the second Person of the Blessed Trinity committed Himself to the human state. And this is the inexpressible reality of grace, which indeed escapes all definition, properly so called, since it is a divine reality.

When a man burdened with cares and discouraged by failures or conflicts in his work ends his day in bitterness and disappointment and some evenings almost in despair, he finds fresh courage for living in the thought of her whom he loves and of the children to whom he is returning. The smile he *knows* to be awaiting in his home, the presence of those with whom he lives, this intimacy of communion—all this suddenly comes back to him as the essential, as his reason for living, as his supreme dynamism.

When the human being, sometimes disheartened almost to the point of despair by misunderstandings, failures and the burdens of daily life, thinks in silence of the absolute unfathomableness of the love toward which he moves by the dim light of faith and hope, with the rest of his brothers, he recovers his zest for life and finds again the profound meaning of his own dynamism.

The quest for balanced living—about which so much is heard in these times—is a movement that does not stop, a journey, a route at once pleasant and deceptive, that one follows but which may lead anywhere. And one can understand that the neurotic depressions, the anxiety crises, the dramatic suicides, are the tragedies of those whom no one helped to find or follow the right route. Just as one can also understand the tragedies, even more dramatic sometimes, of those who have been misled in the matter of religious realities. . . .

Misled, the Mystery of the Lord disfigured by narrow moralism, by fear, by reducing Christ's message to the level of the pharisaical outlook; misled in having had their early years enveloped in an atmosphere that hindered or warped their emotional expansion, and that contradicted the religious practice, sometimes both vital and sincere, of the family environment. . . .

Briefly, the Christian life is one of progressive liberation. It consists in man freeing himself from attachment to the transitory values of this world, values that always tend to assume for him the aspect of the absolute. It consists in laying his soul open to the mysterious action of grace and allowing divine life to germinate within him, the only way possible to the attainment of that perfect co-existence in absolute communion that is to be found in the world of the Resurrection.

All religious education, in its teaching aspect as in the existential atmosphere in which the child grows up, should be centered around the positive power of love and of hope. The mature Christian is a pilgrim who becomes more and more conscious of the Kingdom of God.